MONSTRUM!
A Wizard's Tale.

This is the first publication, **1990**.

Published by
FORTEAN TOMES
1 Shoebury Road, East Ham, London E6 2AQ.

This book was edited and indexed using **Prefis** *Bookmachine* ®
photoset by **D.R. Neaves** of Northampton
and printed and bound
by **Bell & Bain Ltd** of Thornliebank, Glasgow.

British Library Cataloguing in Publication data:

Shiels, Anthony N.   *1938 –*
Monstrum! A Wizard's Tale.
1. Celtic tales
I. Title
398.2'1'094

ISBN   1 870021 04 5

MONSTRUM!
A Wizard's Tale

TONY 'Doc' SHIELS
Introduction by Colin Wilson

FORTEAN TOMES ● LONDON

Dedicated to:

Ruan, Finbarr, Cíara, Louis, Dónal, Aoife

PUBLISHER'S ACKNOWLEDGEMENTS

Fortean Tomes extends its grateful thanks to Janet Bord and the Fortean Picture Library for their help and generosity.

ILLUSTRATIONS

All drawings and photographs are the property of Tony 'Doc' Shiels or from his collection, unless the source or copyright owner is given in square brackets in the caption. ANS denotes Tony 'Doc' Shiels; FPL denotes the Fortean Picture Library.

Reasonable attempts have been made to trace copyright holders of illustrations. Where this has been unsuccessful we invite the owners to contact the publisher.

Cover: Detail from 'Temptation of St Anthony' by Heironymous Bosch, c.1500.
Back cover: Painting by Doc Shiels; detail of Nessie photo taken at Loch Ness, May 21, 1977. [ANS/FPL]

PREFACE   9

INTRODUCTION   11

1   WHERE BE DRAGONS?   21

2   SEA GIANT   27

3   DREAMS AND DAYMARES   37

4   THE OWLMAN COMETH   51

5   MONSTERMIND   69

6   CELTIC CONNECTIONS   85

7   SIGNS AND PORTENTS   97

8   THE PICTISH BEAST   111

9   REVELATIONS   127

BIBLIOGRAPHY   138

INDEX   140

Preface
Introduction

PREFACE

THIS is a book about monsters and minds, portents and paradoxes, sea serpents and surreality. It is riddled with contradictions, objective and subjective; theses, antitheses, and syntheses. Its assertions are tentative. It refuses to take itself too seriously, but insists on the essential veracity of its contents while encouraging a tolerant scepticism towards the notions expressed. Its intentions are honourable.

I make no apologies for personal anecdotal aspects of the text. I have a tale to tell, or, if you prefer it, a yarn to spin. The coloured threads of my experiences, my direct participation in some extraordinary happenings, are twisted together with metallic strands of science and philosophy to form a rope with which, either, to hang myself, or, to perform a kind of conjuring trick. I am, as it happens, something of a conjurer.

Many books (and this could be *the* one too many) have been written on the broad subject of 'strange phenomena'. Some are good, some are bad, and the others are ones I haven't got around to reading yet. From some of those enjoyed and admired I have filched chunks of wisdom and knowledge. Even the bad books contain a lesson or two. I admit to the influence of numerous masters and mistresses in the magnetic fields of zoology, psychology, archaeology, mythology, anthropology, phenomenology, biology, teuthology, etymology, philology, theology, cryptology, and art. I claim no originality for my ideas, though you may consider some juxtapositionings novel and, perhaps, worthy of consideration.

Monsters are, by their very supernature, monstrous. They are abnormal, outrageous, prodigious, shocking and marvellous. They exist to tell us something, but their messages are coded. This book exists to tell you something about monsters. As to its message... you will have to make up your own mind.

My grateful thanks to the following, for a great variety of reasons: Janet and Colin Bord, Tim Dinsdale, Robert Anton Wilson, Robert J.M. Rickard, Graham McEwan, Colin Wilson, David Clarke, Masklyn, Pat Scott-Innes, Kevin McGlue, Dermot and Maeve Maguire, Tim Beattie, Paul Screeton, David Westby, Linda Peet, Mandy Travis, Eileen and Mary O'Donoghue, John Gordon, Mike Truscott, Seamus Creagh, Ashley Drees, Declan King, Serena O'Brien, Pauline Dodds, Skid and Mac, Pam Brogan, Tom Clancy, Lynn Francis, also Chris, Lucy, Kate, Meig, Ewan, & Gareth Shiels.

Tony 'Doc' Shiels.

INTRODUCTION

by Colin Wilson.

I F I had read this book twenty years ago, before I began to develop an interest in the 'paranormal', I must admit that I would have suspected that its author was either a madman or a practical joker. Not, I hasten to add, that I have any doubts about the existence of sea serpents and lake monsters; the evidence is powerful enough to silence any sceptic who takes the trouble to study it.

In 1930, Commander Rupert T. Gould, a retired naval officer, produced a highly convincing work called *The Case for the Sea Serpent*. Three years later, when a new road had been hacked and blasted along the northern shore of Loch Ness, the famous 'monster' sightings began, and have continued ever since. In 1941, the astronomer Willy Ley devoted four chapters of his book *Exotic Zoology* to sea serpents, and left no doubt that he accepted their existence. And in 1965, the Belgian zoologist Dr Bernard Heuvelmans produced his enormous study *In the Wake of the Sea-Serpents*, whose six hundred-odd pages of case histories could cow the most hardened sceptic. But all these writers took the obvious and sensible view that lake monsters and sea serpents are simply prehistoric survivals, like the coelacanth, that happen to have avoided the observation of scientists because they are rare and indisposed to make a show of themselves.

I first became aware that there was an alternative to this view in the early 1970s, when I began a correspondence with angling journalist F.W. Holiday, known to his friends as Ted, who had written a book in which he suggested that the Loch Ness monster was a giant worm (*The Great Orm of Loch Ness*). Early in 1973, Ted sent me his new book *The Dragon and the Disc*, and I was astonished and rather dismayed to learn that he had modified his views, and now seemed to think that the monster – which he had seen three times – was some kind of 'apparition'.

In using that particular word, I admit that I am crudely oversimplifying his suggestions. What he said was that 'by 1970 I had rejected the superficial view of monster phenomena – that they are just unknown animals that have somehow escaped the net of science – as inadequate.' For example, Ted had become increasingly intrigued by the curious ability of the monsters to avoid being photographed. On one occasion he actually had his finger on the button of his camera when the creature plunged below surface. And many other 'monster watchers' have made the same observation. One possible explanation is that the creatures are highly telepathic, as so many animals seem to be, and that its hair-trigger response to danger may explain its survival down the millennia.

Ted had also observed a number of 'unidentified flying objects' (UFOs), and he had also come to the conclusion that these objects seem to behave in a deliberately perverse manner, as if enjoying playing a game of hide-and-seek with their pursuers. Ted concluded that lake monsters may share the contrariness of UFOs and belong to some other order of reality than our every day one. I must admit that I began to suspect that his obsession with monsters had softened his brain.

It was at about this time that I met an extraordinary clergyman named Donald Omand whose views were equally eccentric. I met Donald when I was working as a presenter for Westward Television, and interviewed him on the subject of exorcism. His latest exploit had been to perform an exorcism in a boat on Loch Ness, accompanied by Ted Holiday, on the assumption that the monster was some kind of demonic entity. It had been a pleasant evening as they set out, but within minutes the sky had become overcast and the water choppy. When the ceremony of exorcism was over, both Holiday and Omand felt curiously exhausted...

A few days later, Donald came to stay at my house with his extremely attractive young secretary. We had another guest, a lady from the village, who spent much of her time helping us to look after our children; it was her forthright opinion, after hearing Donald speak at length about ghosts and other such matters, that he was a fake and a dirty old man. I could understand why she thought so – I must confess that the majority of clergy men strike me as con-men – yet I was also fairly certain that Donald possessed genuine powers of 'second sight'. Many of his anecdotes had that odd ring of authenticity that the student of psychical research soon comes to recognize. So, while I was dubious when he told me that he regarded lake and sea monsters as somehow malevolent, I was at least prepared to keep an open mind. After all, it does no harm to refuse to settle for dogmatic opinions.

Soon after the exorcism of Loch Ness, Ted Holiday was walking towards Loch Ness when he saw a man dressed entirely in black standing nearby; he walked past the man, then turned his head and was amazed to find that the man had disappeared. There was no where he could have gone – short of sinking into the ground. A year later, on the same spot, Ted had a heart attack. (UFO *aficionados* will know that mysterious and sinister 'men in black' seem to take pleasure in plaguing investigators.) Five years later, he was to die of another heart attack. Ironically, he had decided against publishing his last book, *The Goblin Universe*, because new photographic evidence of the monster – particularly underwater pictures taken by Dr Robert Rines – seemed to suggest that it was, after all, some prehistoric survival. (By the time the book finally appeared in print in 1986, with an introduction by me, the 'new evidence' had faded, like most of the earlier evidence, into a mist of ambivalence.)

Another friend, John Keel, was to tell me equally strange stories about 'men in black'. John had seen his first UFO in Egypt in 1953, and after undertaking a scientific investigation into the subject in 1966, had been staggered by the sheer number of the sightings, and by the sheer normality of most of the people who reported them. He also heard about 'government officials' dressed in black who visited witnesses and urged them to keep silent. Jacques Vallée, a computer scientist who became interested in UFOs, noted the similarities between stories of men in black and medieval legends about fairies and demonic entities.

In 1967, Keel heard strange stories from West Virginia about a huge winged man who seemed to be able to keep up with fast cars. Keel himself began to have a series of experiences so strange that, if I had not heard them from his own lips, I would be inclined to dismiss them as fantasy. The 'men in black' set out to show him that they could anticipate his every move; on one occasion, he chose a motel at random and found a message waiting for him at the desk. A person who called himself Apol, and who claimed to be one of these sinister entities, began to speak to him through the mouth of a hypnotized 'contactee', and made various prophecies – of plane crashes, of an attempt on the life of the pope, of the assassination of Martin Luther King, of an earthquake in Turkey – all of which came to pass with frightening exactitude.

Keel concluded that Apol – with whom he had many long

telephone conversations – was some kind of 'alien' who did not belong in our space-time frame; in other words, some creature from 'another dimension'. (In 1969, Air Vice Marshall Sir Victor Goddard suggested that UFOs may be visitors from some 'parallel universe'.) When I read Keel's account of Apol in a book called *The Mothman Prophecies*, I was immediately struck by the close parallel between his alien entities and the 'spirits' which so often manifest at seances.

Here I must digress to explain that, when I first began to study 'the occult' in the late 1960s, in order to write a commissioned book on the subject, I expected to find that most of it could be dismissed as fraud and self-delusion. I soon became convinced of the reality of telepathy, 'second sight', even precognition, but was inclined to remain sceptical about ghosts and poltergeists, believing that they could be explained in terms of the powers of the unconscious mind.

By the early 1980s, when I came to write a book on the poltergeist, I had come to accept that these theories were too simplistic. As much as I hated to admit it, I had to recognize that such things as 'spirits' really exist. For the most part, mediums are not frauds or self-deceivers; they are simply 'receivers', like radios or televisions. But the level of the 'communications' seems to depend largely upon the medium herself: if she is an idiot, then she will attract idiots, and the communications are likely to be extremely unreliable. Poltergeists, which manifest themselves through energy 'borrowed' from human beings, are usually little more than juvenile delinquents. I am inclined to conclude that, while he thought he was pursuing aliens from another dimension, Keel had become mixed up in this astral circus, and was simply repeating the experiences of so many amateur mediums of the mid-nineteenth century, when 'table-rapping' suddenly became the favourite party game of every Victorian household (including that of the queen herself).

Now it will be seen why I began to read Tony Shiels' book with interest, then with fascination and absolute absorption. Things that would once have struck me as strange and totally absurd are now seen to be familiar, and totally consistent with what I already know of the subject. Before I was halfway through, I was aware that he had written a book that is destined – like *The Goblin Universe* and *The Mothman Prophecies* – to become a classic in its field.

Who is 'Doc' Shiels? A Lancastrian of Gaelic descent –

(Scottish mother, Irish father – who became an art student in Paris at the age of 18 (in 1956) and also learned the useful art of busking, with which he has supplemented his income over the years. In due course he became a serious and respected painter and has had many exhibitions. He made his first visit to Loch Ness at the age of 20, the year in which he was also married. He became a brilliant stage magician and has written eight books on the subject. But he has always maintained an interest in 'the other kind of magic', the kind practised by the Golden Dawn and various modern groups. In 1976, he was living at Ponsanooth, in Cornwall, when local newspapers began carrying stories of sightings of sea monsters around Falmouth. 'As a working wizard – and, I should add, as a disciple of Charles Fort – it seemed to me a goodly notion that I should hunt, raise, trap and exhibit the beast,' he writes, admitting frankly that his original idea was 'to grab some showbiz publicity by linking myself with the sea serpent.'

He soon realized that he had involved himself in something far more odd than showbiz publicity, and the story of his involvement is told in this literary roller-coaster of a book with a panache and bravura that reveal unmistakably that he belongs to the same race as James Joyce and Flann O'Brien. There are moments when the writing seems suffused with a touch of alcoholic euphoria; understandably, perhaps...

At this stage in the proceedings, I think it would be in order to admit that I am a bit of an old Celt myself. A mixture of Scottish and Irish blood, plus regular lashings of Guinness and whiskey, pursues its eccentric course through my constantly hardening arteries.

... but then, I know him well enough to know that he also talks like this when he is sober. In fact, one of the chief merits of this book is that it conveys the personality of 'Doc' Shiels with almost photographic accuracy – a charm that has nothing to do with Irish blarney, but a great deal to do with an immense natural goodness and amiability.

All this will do nothing to reassure the sceptical reader, who may begin to feel as if he has landed in the middle of an improvisation by Spike Milligan and Harry Secombe. I am afraid I can do very little to help. But let me at least clarify one point. We are not talking about some weird link between sea monsters and 'the supernatural'. The universe that inhabits this

book is fundamentally Jungian, in the sense that it is based upon
the notion of some strange link between the human mind and
the natural world.

In his book on synchronicity, Jung describes how he was
feeling increasingly frustrated by the resistances' of an in-
tellectual woman patient. One day, after she had been recount-
ing a dream about a golden scarab, there was a knocking noise
at the window, and when Jung opened it a green-golden scarab
beetle flew in. The 'coincidence' punctured the patient's ag-
gressive rationalization, and from then on the analysis was able
to proceed more satisfactorily. Jung also recounts a series of
synchronicities in which the image of a fish turned up over and
over again in the course of a single day, at a time when Jung
was studying the meaning of the fish symbol in history.

I found the same kind of thing happening to me when I was
riting *The Occult*, and have described in that book how one day
I needed to look up the meaning of some alchemical symbol, but
felt too lazy to drag myself over to the bookcase on the other
side of my study. However, my better nature triumphed, and I
went to retrieve the book in which I hoped it might be found.
In doing so, I dislodged the book next to it which then fell open
at my feet – at the page I was searching for. Years later, I
decided to write an article on synchronicity for an encyclopedia
of unsolved mysteries. The moment I began to write, the most
absurd coincidences began to occur, some so preposterous as
to be virtually unbelievable. (These are recounted in the article
in question.)

Everyone who has hurled himself into some piece of research has probably experienced something of the sort. And
those who know what I am talking about will also know that it
somehow depends upon being in 'the right frame of mind'.
There is a state of mind that seems to encourage the most
amazing coincidences, and *this* is what 'Doc' Shiels is talking
about in this book. In the later chapters, he makes an attempt
to evolve a theory about such 'coincidences'. Some readers may
well be reminded of Byron's comment on Coleridge...

> *... explaining metaphysics to the nation –*
> *I wish he would explain his explanation.*

It may or may not be significant that *Alice in Wonderland* plays
an important part in this Alice-in-Wonderland logic. Yet for all

its strangeness, I feel that 'Doc' Shiels is making a genuine attempt to get to grips with the problem that caused so much bafflement to Ted Holiday, John Keel and Jacques Vallée. For those who prefer a more rational-sounding approach (and I emphasize the word 'sounding'), I would recommend the last chapter of Holiday's *The Dragon and the Disc* ('An exercise in speculation'), and the last chapter of *Alien Animals* by Janet and Colin Bord ('Following where the evidence leads').

But I suspect that most readers, like myself, will be happy enough to take a trip on the roller coaster, and leave the rational explanations until later.

Colin Wilson

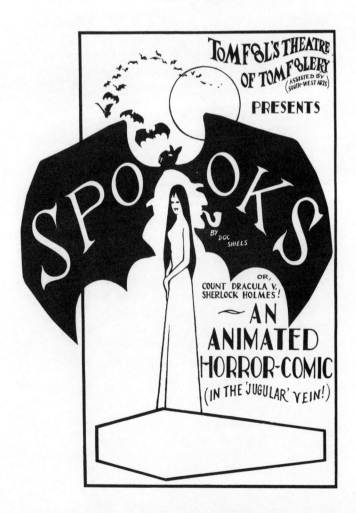

1

WHERE BE DRAGONS?

'The dragon-green, the luminous, the serpent-haunted sea.'
James Elroy Flecker
'And I went out by night by the gate of the valley,
even before the dragon-well.'
Nehemiah, II:13

L ET us begin with a few words about dragons, serpents, and great loathly worms. Grotesquely writhing, coiling, slithering beasts. Treasure-guarding, poison-dripping, fire-spitting monstrosities. Bringers of rain, of thunder and lightning. Dwelling in the deep, damp, dark places of the world, since time began. And now, still, there are dragons.

A potent symbol. The serpent-dragon encircles the earth, as Ouroboros, the 'tail-biter'. Its end is its beginning, forever coiling and recoiling, consuming and renewing, following the cycle of life and death. It is the androgynous mother and father of light and darkness, a synthesis of opposites, active and passive, good and evil, a polyvalent thing.

In Amerindian mythology, the Great Manitou takes the form of a horned serpent, spirit of the fertile waters, a thunder god. To the Aztecs, it was Quetzalcoatl, the plumed serpent, god of lightning, breath of life. In Chinese Taoist and Buddhist symbolism, the dragon represents infinity, sovereignty, spiritual power. In ancient Egypt, a serpent-dragon, Apophis, did daily battle with the sun god, Ra, lord of the sky. The revered Hindu god, Vishnu, rides on giant, multi-headed Antana, ruler of all serpents, whose coils girdle the world. The Babylonian Tiamat, footless dragon of darkness, represents chaos, and is defeated by her son, Marduk, bringer of light. Nidhoggr, the 'Dread Biter' of Scandinavian myth, continually gnaws at the roots of Yggdrasil, the Cosmic Tree; and 'world serpent', Midgard, dwells in the abyss of the ocean, causing storms by writhing its endless coils. A horned serpent, to the Celts, represents Cernunnos, virile 'lord of the animals', and is a symbol of Brigid, the 'Great Mother'. In monotheistic Judaeo-Christian minds, the serpent-dragon is almost totally evil, representing temptation, sin the enemy of God... Satan himself.

The dragon is not simply a mythical monster, an allegorical beast. In certain forms, it was and is believed to exist, physically, as an organic entity. Many familiar living animals have symbolic and totemic meanings: The hare is often connected with lunar deities, a companion of witches. A bull can represent strength and fecundity. A dove carrying an olive branch symbolizes peace and deliverance. The Celtic salmon means wisdom and supernatural knowledge. A fox is the embodiment of trickery and cunning. The list is long, and the majority of symbolic creatures are recognizably real, including, methinks, the dragon.

There are, of course, large numbers of patently *fabulous* monsters, bizarre hybrids, such as the unicorn, gryphon, harpy, basilisk, chimera, gorgon, centaur, cockatrice, etcetera. Things which, generally speaking, have to be believed to be seen. Occasionally, they, or things very much like them... variations on a series of themes... *are* seen, because nothing is absolutely impossible or unbelievable, no matter how fabulous it may appear to be. Serpent-dragons just happen to be rather less exceptional than unicorns, gryphons and so on. They are quite regularly seen, and sometimes even photographed or filmed, by significant numbers of witnesses, suggesting that at least some of these weird creatures have a material existence.

It has to be allowed that some zoologically recognized and not uncommon animals have, in the past, been taken for dragons. Great snakes, crocodiles, and certain schools of queer fish slither into the catalogue of misidentifications.

The greatest snakes alive, accepted by orthodox zoology, are the constrictors: boas and pythons. The Giant Anaconda (*Eunectes murinus*), an aquatic South American boa, is regarded as the largest living snake, reaching a length of thirty five feet or more. The Indo-Malayan Reticulated Python (*Python reticulatus*) is another enormous constrictor, growing almost as long as the longest anaconda. There is an authenticated report of one of these snakes crushing, killing, and swallowing a full-sized bear. In Greek mythology, Python was the name of the serpent killed by Apollo at Delphi, and it has often been misrepresented as a dragon. Pythons are excellent swimmers, and have been observed in lakes, rivers, streams, and even the briny ocean, where the odd specimen may, very occasionally, have been mistaken for a water-dragon or sea-serpent. Real, full-time, sea-snakes, (*Hydrophidae*), are much smaller but more dangerous reptiles than those non-venomous constrictors. India's Hamadryad (*Naja hannah*), the King Cobra, is the world's biggest poisonous snake, and probably the most dangerous of all. Its length sometimes exceeds eighteen feet, and it can kill an elephant. One of its most remarkable characteristics is the power of expanding and flattening its neck, in the form of a hood, when preparing to strike. The Hamadryad and its smaller relation (*Naja naja*) are venerated as serpent-gods in parts of India. Horned serpents, fully accept ed by the herpetological estab-lishment, exist in the forms of African and Egyptian horned vipers (*Cerastes cerastes* and *Cer astes cornutus*), fierce little fellows with convincingly draconic aspects, but far too small to be taken seriously as full-blown dragons.

Crocodiles and alligators are certainly large and dangerous enough to be treated with serious respect. Their sharp-toothed jaws and long crested tails are powerful weapons. They have a reputation as man-eaters. Crocodiles, just like the dragons of legend, lurk in dark holes, tunnelled into the banks of lakes, pools and rivers, below the waterline. Marine Crocodiles (*Crocodylus palustris*) live in the coastal areas of northern Australia and southern Asia. They are especially ferocious, and can reach a length of well over twenty feet. The American Crocodile (*Crocodylus acutus*) is another massive reptile, living in the southern United States and in Central America, which makes a habit of setting out to sea from time to time. Crocodilians have a distinct 'prehistoric' air about them.

Big bad fishes, with sinister reputations and serpentine shapes, are to be found amongst the Anguilliformes: conger and moray eels. Congers (*Congridae*) abound in the Atlantic, Pacific and Indian oceans, the Mediterranean and the Baltic. They are voracious predators. The Conger Eel (*Conger conger*) commonly reaches a length of six or seven feet, and much larger ones have been reported. Morays (*Muraena helena*) are savage eels with large pointed teeth and weirdly menacing eyes. They live in caves and crevices, striking their prey suddenly, like venomous snakes. Morays grow as big as congers.

Smaller than those awesome eels, but much uglier and with far nastier habits, are the lampreys and hagfishes (*Marsipobranchii*). These parasitic creatures fix themselves onto other fishes, usually at the eye or throat, and eat their way, raspingly, inside, devouring blood and muscles. The salivary glands of a hagfish secrete a vampiric anticoagulant, and the animal can eat nine times its own weight in just three hours. When young John Lampton, fishing in the River Wear, hooked a creature 'of most unseemly and disgusting appearance', he caught something very like a lamprey, with nine gill-holes on each side of its 'neck'. Few lampreys or hagfishes exceed a yard in length. The Lampton Worm was, perhaps, a notable exception.

Frightening and ferocious though these beasties be, mankind has known them for millennia. Occasionally, a python, a crocodile, or an especially large eel could be misidentified as a serpent-dragon; but authentic *monsters* are a different kettle of fish, entirely.

Serpent-dragons are to be found, traditionally, in watery places. They dwell in the deep oceans, the fjords and inlets, creeks and coves, the bays and estuaries, rivers and streams, swamps, lakes and pools of the planet. Scotland's celebrated Loch Ness Monster is a typical example: enormous, hump-backed, long-necked, weird, enigmatic. It seems to be a freshwater species of Great Sea Serpent. Similar aquatic monsters are said to exist in many other Scottish lochs, such as Morar, Shiel, Assynt, Arkaig, and so on. Ireland also has a long tradition of monster sightings, at Lough Fadda, Lough Mask, Lough Ree, Lough Conn, Lough Leane, Lough Bran, and scores of others. Lakes in Norway, Sweden, Finland, and Iceland are known to harbour living dragons. Canada has them too, in Lakes Okanagan, Manitoba, Duchene, Simcoe, etcetera. The USA serpent-dragons paddle around Lakes Champlain, Pawaukee, Payette, Iliamna, and a whole lot more. Nessie-like creatures have been spotted in freshwater lakes and rivers of Africa, South America, Russia, China, Japan, and Australia. There are, it seems, a lot of them about.

The Great Sea Serpent has been and continues to be encountered in many salty waters, but most commonly in the North Atlantic. Cornwall's Morgawr is, perhaps, the best known modern manifestation of this perennial maritime giant.

Where be dragons? All over and under the wetter parts of the globe, and in our dreams. I know they exist. I have seen a few myself. I will tell you about them... and some other odd things...

An illustration of two Nessie-like monsters by J.D. Batten, from *Celtic Fairy Tales* by J. Jacobs (1892).

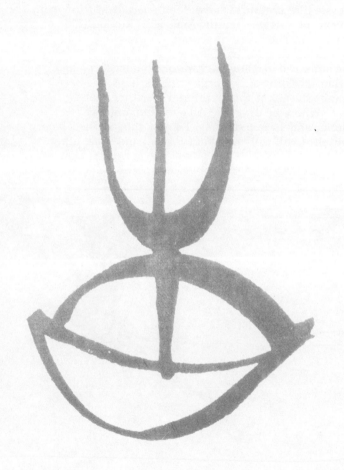

2

SEA GIANT

'It must be the day of the sea sports.'
Ithell Colquhoun
'The blarneyest blather in all Corneywall.'
James Joyce

EARLY in the morning of May Eve, below Mawnan Old Church, by the Helford River, Cornwall, a naked witch draws signs in the wet sand with her staff. She chants words of conjuration in the ancient Celtic tongue of her race: '... *marthys cref yn y nerth ef... Morgawr!*' Then, hands raised above her head, fingers held like horns, repeating the ritual incantation, she walks slowly into the water. The year is AD 1976. The witch is attempting to raise a sea monster. She succeeds.

Six hundred years earlier, another witch sat in the high tower of Pengersick Castle [see pl. 10b] overlooking the cove. She gently strummed a harp and sang strange songs. Great serpents would rise up from the ocean depths at the sound of the Lady Pengersick's bewitching song. She was said to be an Ophidian, a Lamia; and, so legend has it, the weird lady finally cast herself into the sea, where she lives on in serpentine form.

Cornwall is a Celtic country, quite un-English in character and atmosphere, with its own native language. Cornish - Kernewek - is a 'P Celtic' Brythonic tongue, closely related to Armorican or Breton. Although it died out as a first language, over two hundred years ago (Dolly Pentreath, of Mousehole, is popularly thought to be the last native speaker; she died in 1778, aged 102), a great many Cornish words still survive, in place-names, old expressions, tin-mining and seafaring terms, and the names of certain 'things'. One of these 'things' is the *Morgawr*.

Morgawr, sometimes written as *Morgow*, means 'Sea-Monster' or 'Sea Giant', and it is the name by which Cornwall's most famous serpent-dragon is known. Morgawr has raised its ugly head, time and time again, over the centuries, but it was not until 1876 that fable turned into fact when the *West Briton* newspaper reported:

> The sea serpent was caught alive in Gerrans Bay. Two of our fishermen were afloat overhauling their crab-pots about 400 - 500 yards from the shore, when they discovered the serpent coiled about their floating cork (buoy). Upon their near approach it lifted its head and showed signs of defiance, upon which they struck it forcibly with an oar, which so far disabled it as to allow them to proceed with their work, after which they observed the serpent floating about near their boat. They pursued it, bringing it ashore yet alive for exhibition, soon after which it was killed on the rocks and most inconsiderately cast again into the sea.

This was not the end of the monster. In 1882, on 11 October, the Reverend E. Highton reported seeing a large undulating Morgawr off Bude. Just over twelve months later, one of the huge creatures was observed ploughing through the waves off the north coast, at 25 miles per hour. It left a greasy trail behind. During August 1906, Messrs Spicer and Cuming, first and third officers of the trans-Atlantic liner *St Andrew*, plus one of the ship's passengers, Mr P. Hopley, saw an enormous sea serpent as they were rounding Land's End. In April 1907, Mrs J.C. Adkins and her cousin spotted a long-necked, hump-backed monster off Padstow. On 18 September, that same year, the *Western Morning News* reported that some students had seen a Morgawr from Tintagel Head. In 1926, fishermen, Mr Reese and Mr Gilbert, trawling in Falmouth Bay, almost caught a weird 'beaked' creature, twenty feet long; but the beast escaped, tearing their nets. Two years later, on 7 June a monstrous carcase was washed ashore at Praa Sands. It may have been the stinking remains of a Morgawr.

Apparently the species survived and multiplied for in 1934, a Falmouth fisherman saw Morgawr in the bay. Then, during the early summer of 1937, a Mylor woman saw a 'large snake-like creature swimming in the sea' near her home. On 5 July 1949, in the tidal creek of East Looe, Harold T. Wilkins and a friend saw 'two remarkable saurians, fifteen to twenty feet long', just like a pair of Mesozoic plesiosaurs.

A quarter of a century went by, then the Morgawrs returned to Falmouth Bay.

One warm sunny evening in September 1975, a Falmouth lady, Mrs Scott, and her friend, Mr Riley, were enjoying a stroll on Pendennis Point when suddenly, in the clear water below, they noticed a large, hump-backed, long-necked sea monster. It had rounded, stump-like horns on the top of its head, and down the back of its neck, a ridge of short bristles. After a few moments the creature dived, then, shortly afterwards, resurfaced with a writhing conger eel gripped in its jaws. Mrs Scott was struck by the grotesque appearance of the creature and swore that, for as long as she lived, she would 'never forget the face on that thing'.

Just three months later, Mr Gerald Bennett of Seworgan encountered Morgawr in the Helford River. He told the *Falmouth Packet* newspaper that he had spotted the monster near Durgan and, at first, thought it was a dead whale, but then: 'as I drew nearer it started to move away smoothly and I could see it was not a whale, nor like any creature seen around here. I judged that part of it I could see above water was about twelve feet in length with an elongated neck'. Mr Bennett reminded readers that, on a wall of the Dolphin, an old Falmouth pub, long since closed, there used to be a carved model of the sea serpent.

By the beginning of 1976, Morgawr was making regular appearances in the Falmouth and Helford areas. Local fishermen started to blame the creature for low catches or damaged gear, for all kinds of ill-fortune. Morgawr was a bloody nuisance, a *bête noir*, a pest. By thinking along these lines, the fishing community was, consciously or unconsciously, following a long-established tradition. Seafaring men, although practical and courageous, are often profoundly superstitious. To this Celtic crew, Morgawr was felt to be an ominous entity.

At this stage of the proceedings, I think it would be in order to admit that I am a bit of an old Celt myself. A mixture of Scottish and Irish blood, plus regular lashings of Guinness and whiskey, pursues its eccentric course through my constantly hardening arteries. I mention this as either an excuse or a reason for all manner of things.

One day in January, Mrs Kay Payne discovered the remains of a large sea creature on the beach at Durgan, Helford, very close to the spot from which Mr Bennett had seen Morgawr. Instantly dubbed the 'Durgan Dragon', Mrs Payne's monster proved to be the headless body of a whale. Morgawr was still alive and well, and was seen that month, by a dental technician, 100 yards off Rosemullion Head. The witness, Mr Duncan Viner of Truro, described a long-necked creature, with a smooth dark hump, thirty to forty feet overall. Then there was another sighting from Rosemullion about a week later, when Miss Amelia Johnson, from London, and her sister were taking a walk along the coastal path. She described her experience to the *Falmouth Packet*: 'Looking out to sea, I saw a strange form suddenly emerge from the water in Falmouth Bay. It was just like the sort of description one hears of the Loch Ness Monster, a sort of prehistoric monster thing with a neck the length of a lamp-post.'

As a working wizard, it seemed to me a goodly notion that I should hunt, raise, trap and exhibit the beast. This idea was encouraged in letters received from one Professor Michael McCormick [see pl. 12c], of Albuquerque, New Mexico, USA... a kind of latterday Phineas T. Barnum, writ somewhat smallish, sole proprietor of McCormick's Matchbox Circus. Like myself, the professor was a professional showman–shaman, keen to involve himself in what could turn out to be a splendid publicity stunt.

1976 turned out to be Falmouth's 'Year of the Dragon'.

Cornwall's patron saint is Piran, an Irish rover who sailed over on a millstone, like so many of those divine Hibernian gospel-spreaders. His special day is 5 March, which happens to be the day on which my wife and I got married and, perhaps significantly, the day in 1976 when the *Falmouth Packet*, on its front page, published the first photographs of Morgawr. Two black and white pictures had been sent to the newspaper by a woman calling herself 'Mary F'. She refused to give her full name. The photographs [see pl.6] had been taken some time in early February, from Trefusis Point, near Flushing, and clearly showed the dark bulk of a serpent-dragon. In a letter to the newspaper, 'Mary F' described the beast:

> I'd say it was fifteen to eighteen feet long (I mean the part showing above the water). It looked like an elephant waving its trunk, but the trunk was a long neck with a small head on the end, like a snake's head. It had humps on the back which moved in a funny way. The colour was black or very dark brown, and the skin seemed to be like a sea-lion's. I'm glad to know that other people have seen the great Cornish sea serpent. As a matter of fact the animal frightened me. I would not like to see it any closer. I did not like the way it moved when swimming.

The pictures fitted the description, and convincingly showed how the silhouetted creature changed its outline between shots, the neck stretching and curling, the humps undulating. I rushed a copy of the *Packet* piece to Professor McCormick, who swiftly responded with the announcement that he would be heading for Cornwall, pronto, sailing (yes, he chose to come by sea) from New York on 17 March... St Patrick's Day.

McCormick arrived eventually, bringing with him a 'stuffed basilisk' and the skeleton of an 'imp', complete with wings and horns. He gave some newspaper interviews and appeared on television, announcing our dragon-hunting partnership and stating his intention of shrinking the monster, Morgawr, to manageable proportions, by magical methods, and popping it into a bottle for display purposes.

The media did not take him too seriously, and, on Thursday 1 April, All Fools' Day, the *Falmouth Packet*, with the assistance of some local art students, organized a monster prank. This centred around a large, inflated, black plastic, mock-Morgawr which was ceremoniously towed around the harbour by a local trawler for about ten minutes before springing a leak, collapsing and sinking, to the cheers of a fun-loving audience.

After this merry jape, Professor McCormick, feeling somewhat deflated himself, quickly altered his plans and soon waved goodbye to Cornwall.. and Morgawr.

By treating the whole subject as a joke, the press may have caused some important sightings to go unreported and unpublished. The *Packet* stunt must have convinced many people that Morgawr was merely a hoax, a gimmick dreamed up by the newspaper as a short-lived piece of light entertainment. One result of this was that 'Mary F' insisted on maintaining her anonymity.

She had obviously been disturbed by the size and strange appearance of the creature she had photographed, and was not prepared to suffer the inevitable ridicule which would follow the publication of her true name. Various serious and sympathetic investigators attempted to contact 'Mary F', and odd rumours about her possible identity began to circulate within the cryptozoological community. She was said to be a titled lady, a famous spiritualist, or a nun from the local convent. She wrote to the *Falmouth Packet*, explaining that the Morgawr photographs had been developed by her brother, who had sold the negatives to 'an American gentleman'. I also, eventually, received a letter from the mysterious lady imploring me to drop my inquiries concerning her identity. It seemed that, quite unconsciously, I came rather too close for comfort. She told me I could publicize her photographs but not her name. She was, perhaps, being a wee bit over-cautious. I still don't know the full name of 'Mary F', but can tell you that she no longer lives in Cornwall.

Around Easter time that year, as if the cosmic joker wished to stir things up in Cornwall, there was a veritable plague of phenomenal events: Weird lights began to appear in the night sky; an alien entity was seen hovering over an old church; unexplainable noises and smells began to disturb the populace; sightings of assorted 'little people' were said to have occurred; and Morgawr continued to rise from the waters. There was witchcraft in the air.

Cornwall has long been famous for its witches, wizards, enchanters, and pellers. There was Madgy Figgy of St Levan, Old Joan of Alsia Mill, the Witch of Treva, the Witch of Fraddam, Tammy Blee of Redruth, Jimmy the Wizard of Illogan, the powerful Pengersicks, and thirteen devil's dozens more. In the midnineteenth century, Robert Hunt wrote that a 'deep-rooted belief in the power of the witch still lingers in the remote districts of Cornwall.' More than a century later, this belief has become widespread, even fashionable. Building on the evidence for the 'Old Religion' supplied by Charles Leland, Margaret Murray, and others; encouraged and popularized by the writings and doings of Gerald Gardner, T.C. Lethbridge, Michael Harrison, Louise Huebner, Pat Crowther, Alex Sanders, Sybyl Leek, and scores of assorted 'New Age' apologists, 'witchcraft' is thriving. The main impetus came during the 'psychedelic' 'sixties, as part of the hippy movement, when 'alternative' ways of dealing with the world were at the centre of a would-be revolutionary youth culture. Thousands of young people, as part of their protest against 'sick' civilization, took to drugs, cartomancy, ley-hunting, herbalism, astrology, earth magic, numerology, sex magic, and witchcraft. It was the time of Tolkien and Leary, pipe-weed and flower-power.

Cornwall was a haven and hot-bed of hippydom, and this may

have had something to do with the fact that, by 1976, this part of the world was home to a number of practising witches, mainly of the post-Gardnerian, so-called post-Alexandrian, or Paul Huson schools. A few were actually native-born, hereditary followers of pagan Celtic witchcraft. That is to say, their beast-horned 'god' was (is) old Cernunnos, who has great power in Kernow. This power was demonstrated in the spring of 1976.

On the night of Tuesday 13 April, three 'sisters of the craft' got together over drinks in the Red Lion pub, Mawnan Smith, a mile or two from the Helford River. Their witch-names were Amanda, Vivienne and Psyche. Amanda was a local lass; Vivienne was Cornish, too, but had travelled down from London where she had been living for some years; Psyche had come all the way from Inverness, where they know something about monsters. At nineteen, Scottish Psyche was the youngest of the trio, but certainly the most gifted. She was the latest in a long family line of Highland 'wise women', and had learned the secrets of enchantment from her mother. Meanwhile, back in my village of Ponsanooth, I was enjoying a pint at the Stag Hunt. At around ten o'clock, the telephone rang and Mr Richards, the publican, answered it. A few moments later he gave me a mysterious note, hastily scribbled: 'Your weirdest sister says step lively tonight we do a sand dance at the parson's'. The caller was a woman, and Mr Richards swore he had taken her message word for word. 'Didn't know you had any sisters,' said he. 'I don't,' said I. Mr Richards gave me another drink. 'What kind of voice and accent did she have?' I asked. 'Educated,' he replied, seriously.

I sat in a quiet corner of the bar and pondered over my pint. 'Weirdest sister'? Who could it be? Not just weird, but weirder than weird, the weirdest. Weird, weirder, weirdest. The weirdest of three weird sisters. Ah, the 'Scottish Play', that had to be the clue. 'When shall we three meet again...' and so forth. Witches, then, it seemed. Fates, perhaps. 'Step lively' had to mean just what it seemed: step it out or follow in a brisk manner. But 'tonight we do a sand dance at the parson's' had me scotched for a while. I thought of the music-hall turn, the 'Egyptian' sand dance of Wilson, Kepple and Betty, but it didn't help much at the time. Sand, in Cornwall, usually means beaches. This startlingly simple notion eventually popped into my boozer's brain. Witches dancing on a beach. 'At the parson's'? Of course, it was Parson's Beach! This boulder-strewn piece of sand is on the Falmouth side of the Helford River, below Mawnan Old Church [see pl. 10a]. Three witches were obviously about to attempt a conjuration of Morgawr, probably around midnight. I ordered another pint, quite unwilling to 'step lively' at that late hour, with no transport handy. Parson's Beach is at least ten miles from Ponsanooth.

Very early the following morning, with a trusty old camera slung round my neck, I hitch-hiked towards Parson's Beach. Luckily, I was picked up almost immediately from Treluswell Cross and arrived in Mawnan Smith around sevenish. An hour or so later, I was clambering around the boulders on Parson's Beach looking for signs of witchcraft. The top surface of one large rounded rock was scorched and blackened as if from a recent fire. I was preparing to photograph this when I heard a movement, a rattling of pebbles behind me. I turned, and there, quite naked and una shamed, stood a young woman, dripping wet, staring straight at me. I stared back. 'Put that bloody camera down!' she commanded. 'We don't want any photographs.' I meekly acquiesced, noting the Highland lilt in her accent. She had a magical sign painted on her belly, a sign very personal to me, immediately above a place very personal to her. 'Weird sister?' I enquired. 'The weirdest,' she replied, stooping to pick up a hooded black cloak which she flung around her shoulders.

Later, when she was dried and dressed, we climbed up the cliff and followed a wooded path to Grebe where she had parked her car. She told me her witch-name, Psyche, and the names of her two friends. She said that, throughout the previous night, they had conducted magical ceremonies, while three other groups of three witches worked in other parts of Cornwall, to raise the serpent-dragon, Morgawr. Vivienne and Amanda had left at dawn, as the tide turned, to go and meet some of the other witches near Zennor. Psyche stayed behind, to complete their conjurations with another swim, and to meet me. She knew I would arrive sooner or later. I told her that I recognized her name and the sigil she wore. I was meant to. She advised me to spend as much time as possible, that year, eyes peeled, binoculars and cameras at the ready, patrolling the northern bank of the Helford, between Grebe Beach and Rosemullion Head. Sitting in the car, we talked for over an hour, then the Inverness witch-girl drove me back to Ponsanooth, dropping me off near my home.

For some reason or another, I was sure I had met Psyche before, somewhere, in quite different circumstances. The notion nagged, while, for the remainder of that genuinely fateful day, I made careful preparations for a Morgawr hunt.

The game was well and truly afoot.

DREAMS AND DAYMARES

*'Surrealism is based on the belief in the superior reality of
certain forms of association hitherto neglected, in the
omnipotence of dream, in the disinterested play of thought. It
tends to ruin, once and for all other psychic mechanisms and to
replace them in solving the main problems of life.'*
André Breton

W ITCH is an oldish word, which springs from the Old
English *Wicca*, related to Middle Low German,
wicken, to conjure, to change, to turn. It is related to
Wizard, or *wiseard*, a wise one, and *wise*, from the old Frisian *wisia*,
to turn, as in counterclock*wise*, or wither-widdershins.
Wiccaweave, twisted wickerwork and candlewicks. Witches and
wizards change things, turn them into other things, oppose things,
go against the usual round of things. A creepy feeling begins to
creep up on us. In Lancashire, a place of witches, creeping creatures are called 'wick things', which makes me think of Joyce's
Earwicker, in *Finnegans Wake*, and wiggling earwigs, creeping
spirally into the ears of dreamers. *Earwigging*, in archaic usage,
means the influencing of a person's thoughts through insinuation.
Wig-wag zig-zag... wigwam wikiup. For a time, one of my schoolboy
nicknames was 'Earwig'; and, for another time, I lived in Wigtown.
There's a place called Wicca near Zennor.

A wicked Wicklow whiz-kid wished to witness wise wigged
and wizened witenagemot whisk whiskey and wiggling witchetty
grubs in Wichita.

This is a Fortean way to arrive at the start of something
biggish. We call it *lexilinking*, a term coined ringingly by A.J. Bell.
It is a thing which James Joyce spent most of his life doing, which
Charles Hoy Fort [see pl. 13a] enjoyed, and which surrealists will
always do. It sometimes reveals hidden meanings.

Morgawr can be anagrammatized into a wiggling *ragworm*,
which could indicate a giant polychaete of the *Nereis* clan. In Greek
myth, the fifty Nereids were sea nymphs, mermaids, attendants of
the sea-goddess Thetis. If I replace the letter M (for Morgawr) with
T (for Tony), we arrive at *Torgawr*, a giant pile of Celtic rocks, or
ragwort, a wild yellow-flowered plant. Cornish witches traditionally take off from piles of rocks, riding astride stems of ragwort,
using them like broomsticks, for night-flying. Off with the raggle-
taggle witches o! Witches and worts and rags and worms. The

witches used worts to cure ailments, hence the names spleenwort
and liverwort. What of the rag? When I was a lad, 'ragtime' was the
rather coarse slang term for a woman's menstrual period. The
witch's curse... there'll be blood on the moon! It took a wee while
for me to relate it to Scott Joplin's style of music, even though I
played hot piano and all that jazz. I remember, back in 1956, in
Paris... but not yet.

You see, I am trying to give a hint of the thought processes
at work. Rag, tattered, torn piece of cloth, rag-trees near the wells,
and worts and worms, lunatic linkage. Ragman Ragamoffyn is the
very devil in *Piers Plowman*, and a rag is a rough or boisterous joke.
Witchcraft and the demon-worm, Morgawr, one hell of a laugh.
Ragman Joplin, and then there was Janis, pearly thrills. Lytham
and booze? Jan is Janus, two-faced keeper of the bridges, tunnels,
doorways and passageways. No? Scott's the ragtimer's name, and
the wizard's name. Janis, Jan is, Jan is Jan Scott!

My mind boogie-woogied back in time, twenty years, to Paris.
It was there and then that I read the works of Charles Fort for the
very first time. I was painting pictures during the day and making
a living by night, playing blues piano in the rue de la Huchette. It
was also there and then that I met a beautiful young woman, a
painter, whose name was Janet Scott. I called her Jan. She came
from Dumfries, in Scotland, and was in Paris to study. We used to
chat for hours about painting, poetry, surrealism and magic. She
knew more about those things than I did, then. Three weeks after
we first met, I moved down south to Antibes and Jan moved further
south, to Mexico, where she planned to meet up with Remedios
Varo and Leonora Carrington, two surrealist painters.

Psyche, of course, was Jan's daughter.

Magic circumstance, coincidence, objective chance, or something very similar had, in 1974, inspired me to suggest Psyche as
a stage name for one of my own daughters, Kate, who was playing
the psychic, doing a mind-reading act, in those days. It seemed
entirely apropos and suitably showbiz. Kate hated it, preferring to
be known as Kate Shiels, or something of the kind. I had a fair idea
that Jan's daughter knew something about this, and I challenged
her on the subject when next we met.

Lexilinkage had revealed the identity of our Highland witch,
but it still had much more to tell me. Sometimes it takes years for
the messages to filter through, and prove the truth of symbolic
premonitions. I had a worm, a rag, a wort, a witch, a Scot, a pile
of stones, a puzzle. That very morning, I had climbed onto a sea-
sculpted boulder to find the ashes of a ritual fire. There had to be
some meaning in the rocks. Cornwall certainly has more than its
fair share of significant stones, a fact I found daunting. Logan
stones, those rocking rocks, were associated with ragwort-riding

witches. An old rhyme came to mind:

> Robert Rutter dreamed a dream,
> He dreamt he saw a raging bear,
> Rush from the rugged rocks,
> And around the rugged rocks,
> The ragged rascal ran.

That's the original rhyme, or so the scholars say; but who was Robert Rutter, and why was he so ruttish? We shall see, best beloved, we shall see. Robert Hunt tells us how the Cornish giants - Cormelian, Cormoran, Bolster, Holiburn, Trecrobben and all those other titanic gents - used to toss great boulders around for sport, typical Celts that they were, and rearranged much of the granitescape. I wondered, could King Arthur be the 'raging bear'? Stones and swords and bloody sorcery! Did the serpent–dragon, Morgawr, have links with the Pendragon family? I hoped the Holy Grail wouldn't come into it, not being overkeen on holy things of any description, and all that 'quest' stuff embarrasses me.

Arthur, if he existed, was most probably a raging, pagan, bear of a Dumnonian Celt. Arthur, the bear Artemis, the she-bear Artio? Artaios? Art is an Irish bear... but it is the dragon–worm–serpent–things for which we are poking about in Rutter's dream. Did Rutter cut a rut around the rugged rocks? Did he get into one, a rut, that is? Was he a horseman, a rider? We play with the Doctrine of Correspondences. Our real interest here, as Charles Fort put it, 'is not so much in things, as in the relations of things.' Through these relations, deep secrets are revealed.

So Rutter's a rider who rides around rocks, does he ruttingly ride a cock-horse? Does he ride a cock-horse to a cock-crow stone, to see a fine lady, astride a white horse, with rings on her fingers and bells on, of all things, her toes? The topmost stone of the Cheesewring, near St Cleer, turns three times at cock-crow, or so says Robert Hunt. Another Cornish cock-crow stone lies in Looe Harbour, where Morgawrs have been seen. Once upon a time, these stones must have been logan or rocking stones. A cock-horse is a rocking horse or hobbyhorse. Maybe Rutter rode to Padstow in the hoofsteps of St George of Cappadocia, the noted dragon-basher. St George's Well is near Stepper Point just north of Padstow, where Morgawrs have been seen.

By Padstow harbour, there's a money-bank, and, on its roof-ridge, two small horsemen are prancing. They are said to come down and gallop around the streets of the town at midnight. Whimsical folklore. Padstow's most famous horse, the fearsome Obbyoss, is more to our liking. He's a round, black, rocking beast of a thing, and his 'rider' wears a devil mask and tall pointed hat. The Obbyoss is something to be reckoned with; authentically, anciently magical. It is seldom that I have missed being in Padstow on May Day. I used to busk there every year, with conjuring tricks, fortune-telling, and a Punch and Judy Show. Wild-eyed, long-nosed, humpy-backed Punch rides a hobbyhorse, too, and wears a pointed hat. I have painted many pictures of the old 'oss, and Mr. Punch.

There isn't much horse about the Padstow Obbyoss, except its hook of a horsehair tail and a tiny vestigial head. Professor Stuart Piggott would, I think, describe that head, to his students, as *skewmorphic*. Make of the word what you will, but I think a 'skewmorph' is something the shape of which is merely a shrunken and obliquely-viewed reminder of a largely forgotten original. Even the name, *Obbyoss*, retains little of a normal horse, and sounds more like the hobgoblin *Hobyahs*, which gobble people but get gobbled themselves by a big black dog.

Anyway, the Obbyoss is shaped like an over-sized long-playing record, with tarry lappits and a blackened sailcloth skirt. The muscular man inside pokes his head through the centre of this inky flying-saucer, and wears a grinning, sharp-toothed, red-tongued, goat-bearded mask, topped with a wizard's conical hat. Thus, the man is, centaur-like, both rider and ridden. He carries the 'oss and the 'oss carries him. He is, for a time, 'possessed', becoming an integral part of a startling synthesis. This randy rollicking thingumajig traps squealing women under its skirts and they dance a baby-making polka together. In the good old days, Obbyoss men were naked. Who told me? Well, more than one stout fellow, just emerging, sweating, from his ritual exertions under the 'oss. A pint of beer is always welcome at such times.

It would be May Day in just two and a half weeks.

I had spent some hours, that Wednesday, juggling with words (Zounds! I was never so bethumped) and meanings, building up a heap of notes and doodles, filling my brain with a paradoxical bubbling lobscouse of images and speculations. I believed in Morgawr, at least I believed that the people who believed they had seen Morgawr believed in Morgawr, but I desperately desired to see the thing myself.

As a very young child, during World War II, I once saw, or thought I saw, a large, python-sized, swollen, glowing, green, caterpillar-thing, on a bomb-site in Pendleton. It scared the hell out of me. Perhaps it was just, as they say, dismissively, an 'apparition'. Today, I'm inclined to consider it as more of a premonition. It most certainly disturbed my senses; and the thought of it, even now, gives me a weird *frisson*, mainly because of the bomb-site. The image is surreal, in the way that Lautréamont's 'chance encounter of an umbrella and a sewing-machine on a dissecting table' is surreal.

We tend to grow up with certain expectations of objects in

definite situations. 'Normal' perception, survival even, depends on this. When our expectations are banjaxed, by unfamiliar combinations of objects in familiar situations, we experience a feeling of shock or confusion. We are in the habit of abstracting, storing, and reacting to the invariant features of the world. This habit conditions 'normal' perception. Surrealists deliberately encourage what Breton has called a 'perturbation of the intellect', a reeducation of the senses. The process involves a breakdown of 'normal' perception, 'normal' actions and reactions, a rejection of 'everyday reality' with its boring repetitions. The surrealist aim is to experience objects and situations as if they had never 'happened' before, so that even seemingly banal 'everyday' situations and activities become charged with a feeling of the 'marvellous'. Familiar things – shoes, cups, bicycles, trees, horses, clocks, bottles, etc – are seen as if never seen before. The ordinary becomes extraordinary. Reality becomes *surreality*.

I wanted to see Morgawr.

Automatic writing and automatic drawing are ways of cutting through the mantle of dull habit. The results can be either wearisome or exciting. As techniques they are useful but limited. I have never indulged in automatism for the purpose of contacting 'spirits of the dead', or any such nonsense. Spiritualist mediums are, as far as I'm concerned, either charlatans or deluded eccentrics. So-called 'spirit messages' (like UFOnaut messages) are invariably dim-witted. But psychic automatism is, or can be, an important shamanic-poetic activity. It is, of course, merely a variation on the old psychoanalytical method, where a patient is encouraged to relax and go into a rambling monologue. For a writing or drawing experiment, all you need is a good supply of paper and a pen. Then ignore the external, conscious world and allow your internal self to spontaneously scribble, uncensored and unselfcritically, faster and faster. You will enter a kind of (quite unmystical) trance state, and things will most certainly happen. They happened on Wednesday 14 April 1976, when I decided, in the early evening, to simply let mind and pen wander.

After a couple of hours of sometimes quite demented scribbling, I was knee-deep in paper, much of it torn by the frantic, eccentric, high-speed movements of six different pens, all of them finally snapped and broken by the power of muscular psychic automatism. Interestingly, as I just now wrote those few words, by hand, in my first rough draft, the pen began to take on a life of its own and rush along madly for a few seconds. Pure auto-suggestion, of course, but I had to stop, take a deep breath, and consciously control the handwriting at a 'reasonable' readable pace.

To get back to 1976...

The first few pages were not so interesting, and far too

cluttered with obvious references to my thoughts of the previous hours. But I had played this game before and, very soon, slipped into a sort of hypnogogic state. Eventually, the psychomotor was running at such a speed that lines of words became utterly illegible, ripping furiously into the paper. Then, quite unconsciously, writing turned into drawing. Now, I'm quite aware that this sort of thing is 'old hat', but just so long as one doesn't kid oneself that one is making contact with one's dear departed Aunt Fanny, it's a valid activity.

Here, in chronological order, are the six most significant little bursts from that particular session. Please read carefully:

1

clothmothpegi pegeen clouds up on a high cracking jack of all tiradisaboomeranges graze in greatly moveoverstuffyand treesawl meldanlegato eyes eyes right eyes leftright eyes front eyesholeyefulleyeballashes it down.

2

tainmoles toughly bold and skittish tax the toads tools of ding dong tolls dingerdongtrolls dong strontiumphant plangentaganetpoll pollywogadoodledawdleday may fair young fay.

3

Broodicockadoodle alladay teddyboyblewday Roundaroundabantic TOC TIC TODOCROC.

4

Spedomphalomanticopocaprimulgimatic waddalithlillyliddbole cats and carts maid it rite with seabankrook gyrobankomanticoras navywavy oola oopsidays rote it round it.

5

Nightblacknighties blackjarshirts nightwatchbeetles of stowtaggin begginginwigs on the green haywiringunnes heads and tails.

6

Whenthe longonz longon longones cum allongallopalloplopped the trees down the tree sag usits featherly fatherly motherly bellydrumming boys of the boobirdband booberonboronboron fiddlerumderumm dum drumderumdrum......... (The 'drumderumdrum' stuff goes on for a long time then turns into a series of long wavy lines.)

Your immediate reaction? RUBBISH! Well, yes, I can quite understand that viewpoint. However, following the excellent example of Kurt Schwitters, I poked around in the garbage heap and came up with a few wee trashomantic truths.

It is fairly obvious that I had some nursery rhyme-ish rhythms rub-a-dub-diddling around in my skull. Automatic writing, for me, is often a foot-tapping, nid-nodding, sing-along process.

This seems to assist or be part of the flow. Without going into a tiresome step-by-step routine, this is how I initially disentangled some of those ultraportmanteau words:

Section one suggested that 'cloth' or 'clothes', even moth-eaten clothes, which turned into clouds, were pegged up high, by an Irish girl called Pegeen, while she enjoyed the crack with a 'jack-of-all-trades'. Something is grazing as a boomerang possibly whizzes by. Then the pen wants to impatiently 'move over stuff'. The trees 'meld' together 'legato', and there are eyes everywhere. Something is lashed down.

Section two gives us some 'toughly bold' (moun)tain moles. Containing, teasingly, a hint of *Tain bo Cuailgne*, a great Irish saga. Those moles are skittish, and they tax the toad's tools. The toads may be tin-miners because Ding Dong is an old mine in West Cornwall. Then the bell tolls, dingerdong, and a troll shows us his 'dong' which could be similar to a toad's 'tool'. Suddenly the miners are onto firework-strontium, plangent in their triumph, so there's a deep-sounding 'dong'. It all quickly turns into a broomsticky *Plantagenet* called Poll, and she becomes a young frog and joins in the old banjo-picking, black-face minstrel song *Polly Wolly Doodle*, dawdling on May Day with a fair young enchantress.

The third section continues the 'doodle all the day' theme. Teddy-boy may be a male bear cub. 'Boy Blue' is in there too, going round and round to the sound of a ticking clock. It ends with 'Doc', that's me, on a rock.

Section four begins with a long and peculiar word which appears to involve speed, the 'omphalos' stone, a romantic cop, a goat and/or goatsucker, all thrown together for some purpose. Lillith waddles in with a lidded lily in a bowl, followed by a cart full of cats who make it right, or write, or to the rite, with money from a seaside Giro-Bank dole cheque, and some naval manticores with hula-hoops. They wrote out the cheque and bought a round.

My fifth begins with naughty black nighties and nightshirts. Black jars must be pints of Guinness, because that stout is quickly mentioned again, and 'gunnes' which makes you go haywire, head over heels, and into an argument, so there are 'wigs on the green', a very old expression.

Number six is the final one, before the words turned into something else. It says that when the long gone ones come galloping, they will lop the trees down. The father and mother of the fat-bellied drummer-boys, in a big-breasted girls' band, bang their drums as a fiddler plays, and they go drumming all the way to the pictures... the pictures being what came next.

They contain a lot of whorls and spirals, doodled at high speed, often in a continuous line, stopping here and there in angry scribbles. Repeated motifs are waves, zig-zags, figures with raised arms and large hands, and a 'thing' which I now recognize as a cephalopodic monster. I reproduce just three, in no special order, and leave detailed interpretation to those readers who enjoy that sort of thing.

At around eleven of the night, my wife and I sat down to supper. I was weary after a long day, but suddenly snapped into wide-eyed wakefulness when Chris, quite casually, made some remark about a full moon. Tonight was the night! To a witch, the full moon represented power. I had been invited to take part in the previous night's 'preparations' because it was the 13th of the month

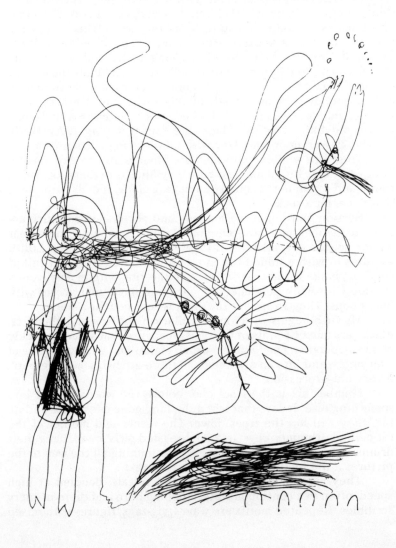

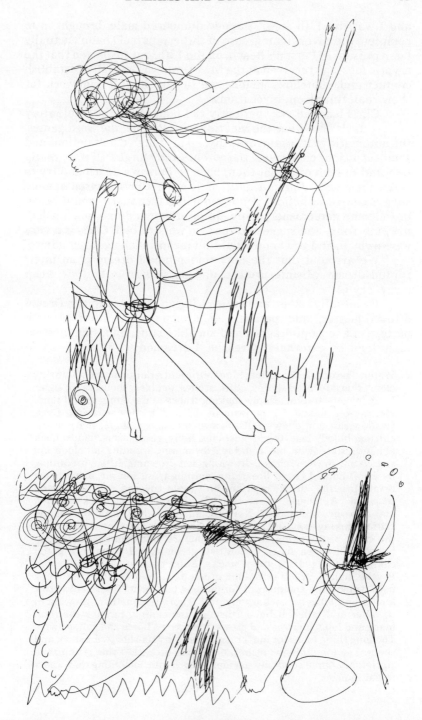

and I was the 13th guest, the odd-numbered male, brought in to complete the coven. Four groups of three, plus me! I hadn't actually been present at Parson's Beach, on the 13th, but suspected that the cryptic message received at the Stag Hunt was enough to establish contact and, somehow, include me in the ritual groundwork for their real, full moon, invocations.

Chris listened very patiently as I poured out the whole story of that day's activities, the meeting with Psyche, the word games, the automatic writing and drawing, all my tangled half-notions and semi-suspicions concerning the witches and Morgawr. I was greatly tempted to rush off, right then, back to Parson's Beach and try to catch them at it, *flagrant délit*, as it were. Chris advised against such a course of action, pointed out the fact that I would be an unwelcome gatecrasher, a spy, an interfering, dumb, pig-headed, peeping Tony, and suggested that we went to bed. Chris is a very *wise woman*, and you know what that means. I followed her advice.

We are told that the only remembered dream is an interrupted dream. Misinterpreters, and persons from Porlock, keep away, say I.

Eventually I slept, and my eyes began to move rapidly. Dream affects matter, and patterns of dream-energy interfere with patterns of serpent-dragons and suchlike stuff, imposing internal night-logic on external day-reason. I dreamed:

Water. The ocean, the rolling blue Celtic and Atlantic waters. Blue sky, clear, sharp-focused shores, cliffs, stones, pebbles, shells, sand, signs. Long-leggety stalking things making tracks in the damp strand sand. Me, myself, naked, I run, swim in the now muddy sea, sink, float, swallow salt and chew shells. Seaweed clinging, slime, sharp shells cutting, bloody legs, thighs, testicles, belly, chest, arms, hands. Look at hands, sink, swim, blood and sea. Swimming, treading salt blood and salt water, swallow, choke, drowning, not drowning, lifted, breathing, by a soft-bodied beast. Breathing, gulping fresh salt air, drink black drink, breathe, drink, breathe. Pub table covered with shells and seaweed. Apologise to crowd of critics. Laugh, mock-casually, embarrassed, still naked. Now, instantly, clothed, I am one of the critics, looking at myself in a picture which falls and shatters. I am still the critic, still looking at a broken picture, but I am me, in a green tweed suit, green shoes, green hat, green skin. I chew on a green calabash pipe, puffing green smoke. Enter twin witches, Psyche and Psyche, naked, green skin, long green hair. They laugh at me. They both drink pints and pints of Guinness. I pay for it. Their necks grow longer and longer. I pick up my pint. There is something growing in it, taller and taller, it bursts through the ceiling, through the roof, black and long. It grows and grows. I jump on a horse and gallop away. The long thing looks for me. I turn, aiming my six-shooters, I shoot and shoot. The long thing vanishes, but it will be back. I ride off into the sunset. My horse suddenly decides to turn into something that wants to eat me.

Surrealchemy – oneiromantically proposed by Max Ernst.
[Ernst, *La Femme 100 Têtes*, 1929]

I wake up. Chris wakes up. 'What's happening? What's the matter?' she asks, and gives me a hug.

I have outlined the dream, starkly and plainly, as I remembered it, unembellished; but, as Freud says, 'what we remember of a dream and what we exercise our interpretive arts upon has been mutilated by the untrustworthiness of our memory'. However, the contents and memory of dream are associatively linked, so memory provides only a thin distortive disguise. As a surrealist, familiar with Freudian symbolism, I reject the psychic censor, as far as possible. This particular dream confirmed my suspicions about the sexual nature of dragon-raising. Very early that morning, I had a hypnopompic vision of Sherlock Holmes and Alice, erotically adventuring, underground.

During the next couple of days, I patrolled the coast around the mouth of the Helford River, between Rosemullion Head and Porthallack, establishing 'observation posts' at Toll point, Parson's Beach and Trerose.

Some funny-peculiar things were happening.

THE OWLMAN COMETH

'An habitation of dragons, and a court for owls.'
Isaiah, 34:13

ON the warm bright morning of Easter Saturday, Mr and Mrs D. Melling, from Preston, Lancashire, were enjoying a Cornish holiday. They had travelled down the previous Thursday evening, with their two young daughters, June and Vicky, aged 12 and 9 respectively. The family had just been exploring the area around Mawnan Old Church, and, while mother and father returned to their car, parked by the church gates, to prepare a picnic lunch, the girls stayed in the sunny churchyard, playing amongst the gravestones. Within a few short minutes, the peace was shattered by terrified screams. Mr and Mrs Melling looked up to see June and Vicky running towards them as if the devil himself was at their heels. Perhaps he was. The girls were quite hysterical with terror, and their parents could not get a word of sense out of them until they were locked safely in the car and quickly driven miles away from Mawnan to their caravan site near Truro.

I met Mr Melling later that weekend at a 'steam fair' near Penryn. It was a get-together of vintage traction engines, plus stalls and side-shows, and I was there with my wife, our daughters, and a couple of friends. A jolly outing on a pleasant day, with the chance to earn a few bob with my busker's bag of tricks. We had just packed up after a conjuring show, and were licking ice-cream cones, tapping our feet to the evocative strains of a giant fairground organ, when a worried-looking man approached. He asked if I was Doc Shiels, the 'monster man', and when I admitted to this, he introduced himself as Don Melling and told me a weird story.

Back at their campsite, when Don and his wife eventually managed to calm their frightened daughters, they asked June and Vicky what had scared them so. The girls said that, when they were playing in the churchyard, they heard a 'funny noise' above them and, looking up, saw a bizarre winged figure, a big feathered bird-man, hovering over the church tower. It was man-sized, with pointed ears and a gaping mouth. At her father's request, June drew a picture of the grotesque apparition. Don gave it to me [see next page].

Don Melling hoped I could explain just what the hell was going on. He had heard about the Morgawr sightings, about my plans to 'conjure up' the sea serpent, and about McCormick and his 'winged imp'. He angrily accused me of setting up some sort of contraption, at Mawnan Old Church, with the intention of terroriz-

ing innocent children. It took quite a while to convince him that
this was not so. Chris and our daughters finally tipped the scales
in my favour. I asked Mr Melling if I could speak to his girls, but
he would not allow this because June and Vicky were still very
upset. The Mellings had hoped that the fair would take their minds
off the Mawnan 'thing', but it had not, and they were going home
next morning, cutting short their holiday by three days, to get away
from darkest Cornwall and its demons.

June and Vicky had, of course, witnessed the anomalous
entity which soon became known as the Owlman. Theirs was by no
means a unique encounter. Peculiar winged things, bizarre
birdmen, and various kinds of feathery frighteners have been
around for centuries. Fortean literature is full of reports concerning them, and flapper flaps happen all over the world, the USA
seeming to be particularly prone to this sort of phenomenon.
During 1976, while Owlman was doing his stuff in Cornwall, the
state of Texas was haunted by a 'Big Bird' with a 12-foot wingspan
and large red eyes in a 'monkey-like' face. Ten years earlier, the
mysterious 'Mothman' – a grey-feathered, luminous red-eyed,
squeaking monster – had upset the good people of Point Pleasant,
West Virginia.

Owlman is just one of the latest in a long list of winged
humanoids. The American Indians have their man-eating Piasa, the
Sumerians feared owl-winged Lilitu, Japan's Tengus haunt the
mountain forests, India has the sacred Garuda, New Zealand's
Maoris tell of all-seeing Pouakai, and the Greek Harpies are a
horrid flock of snatchers.

The Mawnan Owlman as seen by
June Melling, 1976. [FPL]

Demons are often depicted as winged things, and witches are said to consort with demons. Is the Owlman a demon... or, maybe, a *daemon*? I suppose so.

The night after Owlman hovered over Mawnan Old Church, enigmatic coloured lights were seen performing all manner of aerobatics in the Cornish sky. UFO activity continued throughout the year, and was sometimes linked with sightings of Morgawr. The aerial phenomena did not concern me unduly. On almost any clear night, in this part of Cornwall, one is likely to see strange-seeming lights in the sky. Most of them probably originate from the Royal Navy Air Base, Culdrose. Others may be caused by the electrical pylons supporting overhead power lines. A few could be geophysically generated, piezoelectric special effects. One or two may even be alien space craft. Whatever they may be, and the choice is wide, they do not interest me greatly. I have seen some quite spectacular flying 'objects', which I have been unable to identify, but the sight of them has never really excited or profoundly affected me, so far as I know. I tend to take them for granted, which may be foolish, but there we are. Just regard this as a personal quirk. Suffice it to say that these things are seen, and sometimes they show up at the same time as monsters. They form part of the pattern.

Apart from the UFOs, mysterious rumblings, muffled explosions, hummings and cracklings resounded in the air during the spring and summer of 1976. Nasty sulphurous stinks as well. Remember, though, it was the longest hottest summer for many a year, and many of these effects must have been perfectly 'natural', given the unusual weather conditions. Others may have been 'supernatural', particularly the 'crackling' sound heard in trees on the banks of the Helford River. I draw no line between the 'natural' and 'supernatural', and take these phenomena to be interrelated aspects of the whole surreal 'monster experience'.

It was an odd kind of Easter, that year. I decided to spend Saturday night in the Mawnan woods, to keep an eye on things and, with luck, maybe even snap a portrait of the Owlman. After a few 'nightjars' in the Red Lion, Mawnan Smith, I walked down to the Old Church, armed with a camera, electric torch, whiskey flask, sleeping-bag, and a wizard's stick made from the dried core of a New Mexican cactus. Settling myself down, comfortably, against one of the gnarled old trees on the slope below the church, I sat and waited for something to happen. Alert and expectant for the first half hour, I soon nodded off into slumberland, snoring whiskey-scented lullabies to any night-beasts which may have been lurking in the vicinity.

The fearless monster-hunter woke up at dawn, with a stiff neck, a thick head, and an urgent desire to empty his bladder. That accomplished, my next idea was to climb down the cliff to the water's edge and rinse the cobwebs out of my eyes. As I began to descend the slope, there was a peculiar crackling sound in the treetops, probably caused by the morning sun drying the uppermost branches, or pine-cones popping open, or something else entirely. Then, on reaching a rocky ledge, I heard female voices coming from the beach below. One of the voices was Psyche's. She seemed to be intoning something in Gaelic, but I couldn't catch nor understand the words. The other voice responded to Psyche's chant with the repeated English phrase: 'So mote it be'. I crouched behind a clump of furze and peered between its prickles at the theatrical scene beneath me. Psyche and another girl, naked, arms raised, waded into the water, then began to swim. They moved in wide circles, Psyche to the left and her friend to the right. I lost sight of Psyche, but watched the second witch as she continued to swim, round and round, with slow easy strokes.

I decided to go back up the slope and get my camera. If these women, with their witch-skills, succeeded in raising Morgawr, or any other monster, I wanted a photograph of the event. So, as silently as possible, I clambered up the hill and grabbed my old Rollei, returning to the bushy 'hide' moments later. There was still no sign of Psyche, but the other girl was just coming ashore. I aimed my camera in her direction, and the thought crossed my mind that I could probably be arrested for voyeuristic activities. The sky-clad witch was enjoying the warm sun drying her skin. She stood on a large rock, and appeared to be quite unconcerned about her nakedness, caring nothing about being seen, on an Easter Sunday morning, almost as if she was posing for photographs. So I took some, noting, with interest, that my model wore that special sign on her belly, and wondering, vaguely, what had happened to Psyche. Suddenly, I felt guilty and embarrassed. Closing the camera case with trembling fingers, I quickly climbed back up the hill, picked up my gear, and fled.

A couple of hours later, I was gazing across the sparkling river mouth from my 'observation post' near Trerose, camera at the ready, wishing that I owned a 35mm SLR with a telephoto lens. It was all very well being in the right place, but if it turned out to be the right time for Morgawr to appear, my antique Rollei with its standard lens was not the ideal instrument with which to capture the beast for posterity. Pondering photography, I invoked a photographer.

'Hello,' said a voice, and there stood a schoolboy in a schoolboy's blazer. He looked about thirteen or fourteen. 'You're Doc Shiels,' he told me, and I nodded, philosophically, having been told the same thing a thousand times before. 'Hello,' he said again, 'I'm Andrew.' I nodded again, believing him. Andrew carried an impressive-looking 35mm SLR camera with a telephoto lens. For a split second, I considered mugging him and stealing it. No, of course I didn't. 'Hello, Andrew. Where did you spring from?' I asked amiably. 'Helston,' he replied, deadpan, and I laughed. Andrew remained impassive. 'I've been watching you,' he said. My smile faded as another wave of guilt and embarrassment washed over me. The spy spied upon, the voyeur viewed. Cheeky bugger, I thought. 'You're looking out for that sea monster,' he observed, and I smiled again, nodding again. 'That's right,' I told him, 'but I've had no luck so far.' Andrew looked me straight in the eye. 'I've seen it,' he said, 'and I got a photograph of it.' He reached into one of his blazer pockets and produced a large postcard-size monochrome print. 'It's a bit blurred,' he said, handing me the picture. He was right.

The schoolboy's fuzzy photograph showed two black humps and a sausage shape, against a pale off-white background. It was quite unconvincing as a picture of a monster, but I asked the lad if I could borrow it. He told me I could keep it and show it to my 'expert' friends. Andrew claimed to have taken the photograph four days earlier, when he saw Morgawr swimming between Toll Point and The Gew, near the mouth of the Helford. I strongly suspected that I was being set up for a schoolboy prank, and so remained non-committal. I asked Andrew for his full name and address, but he wouldn't tell me, saying that his father would be angry if he did. Andrew gave a leering wink and left me thinking, again, cheeky bugger!

A few nights later, the dubious photograph appeared on a BBC TV 'Spotlight' programme, illustrating a jokey item on Morgawr.

I sent my print to Bob Rickard who, correctly, also found it 'unconvincing'.

Back to Easter Sunday. Around midday, I shifted like a paradigm and headed for the Red Lion at Mawnan Smith. There I found Psyche, sitting at a table in a quiet, cool corner. She had a pint of Guinness ready for me. The witch girl told me that she knew I had spent the night in the woods. She knew I had watched her and Vivienne - yes, it was Vivienne - taking their sky-clad dip. She knew I had photographed Vivienne, who had deliberately stayed behind and posed for the pictures, while Psyche was doing 'other things'. She knew about the Owlman, and the crackling trees. I asked her what else she knew, and she told me there were fairies at the bottom of the garden.

Before we discussed the little people, I told Psyche a few things that I knew. For instance, I knew something about witchcraft and magic; I knew that she and her friends had been up to their tricks on the night of the full moon; and - clever old me - I knew her mother was Jan Scott. Of course, she knew that I knew these things before I told her. We had another couple of jars, and Psyche told me that her 'real' name was Pat Scott-Innes; that her mother

and father, Bob Innes, lived in California; and that I would see
Morgawr before the end of the year. I wanted to know why Pat had
chosen the witch-name 'Psyche', and was it anything to do with the
fact that my daughter, Kate, had used it ; as a stage-name. Pat
admitted that she knew about Kate, but her main reason for picking
the name 'Psyche' was because of her initials: P.S.I. (The following
year, I pinched Pat's initials for monster-raising purposes, so, as far
as name-swapping is concerned, we are all square.) Then she
showed me a photograph of some fairies [see pl. 14c].

According to Robert Hunt, 'there are in Cornwall five
varieties of the fairy family, clearly distinguishable'. These are the
Small People, which are just that, and getting smaller all the time;
the Spriggans, an ugly lot and very tiny, though they can expand
to great size; the Piskies, who have pointed ears and dress in green;
the Buccas or Knockers, imps of the tin and copper mines; and the
Brownies, hairy fairies who often help with domestic chores. Now,
I believe in fairies and I don't care who knows it. Not the pretty
wee, butterfly-winged, sugary sprites of kiddies' picture-books, but
the earthy and sometimes sinister, small supernatural beings of
ancient and modern folklore. I have met people, in this part of the
world, of less than average stature, who, quite seriously and
proudly, claim to have 'pisky blood' in their veins. Cornwall's St
Neot may have come from fairy stock, he was only fifteen inches
tall. Gold and silver 'lucky charms', in the forms of piskies, Joan
the Wad and Skilly-widden, are worn by believers. 'Laughing like
a pisky' is still a common expression. Old mine workings are still
haunted by Knock ers. Twentieth-century Cornish fairies have
been seen flying miniature airships and driving little cars. The
really up-to-date ones travel by UFO. Big people still see Small
People, but often mistake them for 'visitors from space'. What fools
these mortals be!

'Fairy' is a relatively recent word, derived from 'Fay-erie',
meaning the enchantment of Fays or Fates. Morgan le Fay played
the role of bad fairy, or witch, in Arthurian legend, and is linked
with the shape-shifting Irish Morrigan. Fays are human size, but
the term 'fairy' is usually used to describe all classes of diminutive
humanoid entities: Elves, Goblins, Boggarts, Leprechauns, Trolls,
Dwarves, and so on. In a Celtic context, it is, perhaps significant
that etymologists have linked Piskies with both Picts and Pygmies.
In the Scottish Lowlands, the Wee Folk are often referred to as
Pechts. It is no great jump from Pisky to Pooka and from Pooka to
Puck. These elemental earth or nature spirits, aboriginal midgets,
and shape-shifting personeens are known, now, collectively, as
fairies. I have seen them. As a child, on both sides of the Solway
Firth, when I lived at Silloth and Isle of Whithorn, I played amongst
the dunes with these 'good people'. When I was but a wee small lad,

a Mayo lass called Kitty Carroll introduced me to the *Daoine Sidh*. I *know* the fairy race exists, and anyone who denies the fact is, for sure, an ignorant blind fool.

In 1917, at Cottingley Glen, near Bingley, Yorkshire, two young cousins, Frances Griffiths and Elsie Wright, were in the habit of playing with fairies. One day, during a game with the little people, Frances fell in the beck and got a soaking. She was severely reprimanded for the wetness of her clothes and the unbelievability of her excuse. Elsie, bright enchantress that she was, decided to back up the story with photographic proof. She borrowed her father's quarter-plate box camera and, back in the glen, snapped the first of those famous 'Cottingley Fairy Photographs' [see pl.15]. The rest is Fortean history.

Along with many others, I have always thought that the Cottingley sprites, as photographed, were cardboard cut-outs, and it is really rather amazing and amusing that anyone was ever fooled by them; but Elsie knew what she was doing. Her painted pasteboard models were just decoys, and the real fairies encouraged her in an interesting game. The fake fairies of Cottingley were a 'blind'. As Charles Fort may have expressed it, I did not believe in Pat's fairy photograph any more than I believe that two and two invariably make four.

Abruptly, the witch decided to leave.

On the morning of May Eve, I was on Grebe Beach, along with a crowd of reporters, photographers, and two television crews. The word had been put out that pretty young witches were to be seen in the area, disporting themselves in the nude, and the media men decided, wrongly, that I was the impresario behind the entertainment. When naked girls failed to appear on Grebe Beach, the journalists became quite despondent and started to blame each other for scaring the witches away. Then they turned on me, demanding explanation for the non-event. In the middle of a TV interview, a sudden yell went up, I was grabbed by the collar and shoved into an outboard motorboat, leaving the BBC man to 'fill in', as I found myself roaring over the Helford, with a pack of excited newshounds [see pl. 8b], towards the southern bank where a sky-clad witch had just been seen emerging from the water. She disappeared into the trees, a few seconds before we landed. Her vanishing act was complete and quite baffling. The newspapermen spent the rest of that day witch-hunting. One of them was eventually successful.

I crept away, back to Ponsanooth. Later, around midnight, I lit a bonfire and beat my bodhran.

May Day, and the Shiels family, Tom Fool's Theatre of Tomfoolery, Punch and Judy, and the dog Toby, were all in Padstow. The Obbyoss drummers echoed the invocational beat of my bodhran, all around that flowery greenery bedizened town. There was an old-magical air about the place, and a breeze to enliven our fire-spitting. Some dragons would be raised, with the help of old 'Oss, Oss, wee-Oss'.

> Arise up, Miss Scott-Innes, all in your smock of silk,
> For summer is come unto day,
> And all your body under as white as any milk,
> In the merry morning of May.

I met Pat in the evening, at a Wadebridge pub. She told me that the Morgawr had been successfully invoked, and that I would see it before the end of summer. We agreed to work together in the future.

On 4 May, two London bankers, Tony Rogers and John Chambers, were fishing from the rocks at Parson's Beach when: 'Suddenly, something rose out of the water, about 150 or 200 yards away. It was greeny-grey in colour, and appeared to have humps. Another smaller creature also appeared. They were visible for about ten seconds and looked straight at us.' Thus spake Tony Rogers. John Chambers missed the second, smaller Morgawr.

Oh, that 'jollyrodgered sea'. That 'unplumbed, salt enstranging', that 'wine-dark', that 'serpent-haunted' sea. It has been an obsession for most of my life. I have paddled and piddled in it, fished and farted in it, sailed and swum in it. The sea has maddened me. I bottled a pint of the briny stuff and, madly, talked to it, day after hot summer's day. At night, I whispered spells into a spiralling mollusc shell, then listened as the sea whispered back, secretly informing.

Tim Dinsdale, dedicated monster-hunter [see pl. 18], visited Falmouth to investigate the reports of Morgawr. We became good friends.

On Midsummer's Day, three witches, Amanda, Isobel and Brigid performed an invocation ritual at Parson's Beach. I was with them. We worked together as a shamanic team.

On 1 July, at 12:30 am, three fireballs were seen over the Carrick Roads.

On 3 July, around 10:00 pm, the Owlman reappeared. Two young girls, Sally Chapman and Barbara Perry, were camping in the Mawnan woods. They heard a weird hissing sound and suddenly saw the bizarre winged thing amongst the trees, just twenty yards away. Sally, describing it, said: 'It was like a big owl with pointed ears, as big as a man. The eyes were red and glowing. At first I thought it was someone dressed up, playing a joke, trying to scare us. I laughed at it, we both did, then it went up in the air and we both screamed. When it went up you could see its feet were like pincers.'

Barbara confirmed her friend's story: 'It's true. It was horrible, a nasty owl-face with big ears and big red eyes. It was covered in grey feathers. The claws on its feet were black. It just flew straight up and disappeared in the trees.'

I met Sally and Barbara on 4 July, at Grebe, and they told me their tale. Separating the two girls, I gave each of them a page from my sketchbook, and a pen, and asked them to draw portraits of the Owlman, as they remembered 'him'. These were the results:

Top: The Mawnan Owlman as seen by Barbara Perry, and (**right**) by Sally Chapman. [FPL]

Impossible, isn't it? Like something created by Max Ernst, who died in 1976. Owlman of ill omen? That very morning, as we found out later, another two girls, the Greenwood sisters, on holiday from Southport, had seen Owlman near Mawnan Church. Jane Greenwood told the *Falmouth Packet*:

Angst in Mawnan Woods, as foreseen by Max Ernst.
[Ernst, *Une Semaine de Bonté*, 1933.]

'It was in the trees standing like a full-grown man, but the legs bent backwards like a bird's. It saw us and quickly jumped up and rose straight up through the trees.

My sister and I saw it very clearly before it rose up. It had red slanting eyes and a very large mouth. The feathers are silvery grey and so are his body and legs. The feet are like big black crab's claws.

We were frightened at the time. It was so strange, like some thing in a horror film. After the thing went up there was crack ling sounds in the tree tops for ages.

Later that day we spoke to some people at the camp-site, who said they had seen the Morgawr Monster on Saturday, when they were swimming with face masks and snorkels in the river, below where we saw the bird man. They saw it underwater, and said it was enormous and shaped like a lizard.

Our mother thinks we made it all up just because we read about these things, but that is not true. We really saw the bird man, though it could have been somebody playing a trick in a very good costume and make-up.

But how could it rise up like that? If we imagined it, then we both imagined the same thing at the same time.

It was a sizzling hot Sunday, and the Shiels family was spending as much time as possible in the waters of the Helford. After a lively bout of aquasports, we sat on the beach and, from time to time, I scanned the river mouth in case Morgawr should decide to appear. Suddenly, I saw it! But it quickly vanished. Moments later, it was back, and I caught a brief glimpse of two dark humps, about four hundred yards away. As soon as I tried to focus my binoculars on the thing, it disappeared like a phantom. When I looked away, up it came again, a long neck, which teased the periphery of my vision, then melted away when I attempted to look straight at it. Morgawr was playing a game of 'now you see me, now you don't', performing a cunning piece of prestidigitation or sleight of sight, hoodwinking me entirely. I thought I was probably hallucinating, as a result of too much sun or a too urgent wish to spot the creature. Then the others saw it. Chris later told the *Falmouth Packet*:

... the kids started pointing and yelling, 'there it is... the monster!' Finally I saw it (or them) for myself. It was at the edge of my vision and when I tried to focus on the image it simply and suddenly wasn't there. After two or three attempts to get a clear picture of the thing, by staring at it, failing each time, I decided to allow it to be coy, to stay in the 'corner of my eye' so to speak. This worked. For several seconds I saw a large, dark, long-necked, hump-backed beast moving slowly through the water, then sinking beneath the surface.

I was not entirely convinced that we had actually seen a real live sea monster. Visual perception is a matter of interpreting patterns according to our knowledge of 'objects'. We tend to see what we believe. Hermann von Helmholtz, the German physicist, wrote:

The psychic activities that lead us to infer that there in front of us at a certain place there is a certain object of a certain character, are generally not conscious activities, but unconscious ones. In their result they are equivalent to a conclusion, to the extent that the observed action of our senses enables us to form an idea as to the possible cause of this action; although, as a matter of fact, it is invariably simply the nervous stimulations that are perceived, that is, the actions, but never the external objects themselves.

Is, or was, Morgawr, as 'seen' by me, an external object, or something else? What is the connection, if any, between the sea serpent and the eerie Owlman of Mawnan? Both monsters were certainly surreal, but were they linked in any other way?

Later that week, two Falmouth fishermen, John Cock and George Vinnecombe, met Morgawr twenty-five miles south of Lizard Point. Mr Vinnecombe told *Cornish Life* magazine:

We were fishing over wartime wrecks in the channel. It was a beautiful calm, clear day. I looked over the starboard side and saw this thing in the water. I thought it was a boat upside down. We went over to investigate and it looked like the back of a dead whale but with three humps and about eighteen or twenty feet long. The body was black but a lighter colour under the water. Then suddenly this head came out of the water about three feet from the body. It just looked at us and my mate and I just looked at one another. He said, 'What the hell have we got here?' Then the head vanished and the body sank away. I've been fishing for forty years and it's the first time I've ever seen anything like that. Folk have told me about monsters and I always took it with a pinch of salt, but now I'm prepared to believe anything I see out there.

On 11 August, Patrick Dolan, an art historian from Cardiff, was sailing from Falmouth to Kinsale in his yacht *Daisy*. About thirty miles NNW of the Scilly Isles, he encountered Morgawr. Mr Dolan told the *Falmouth Packet*: 'I could see quite distinctly a kind of worm-like shape in the water and the neck was about eight feet out of the water. It was about forty feet long and propelled itself with an undulating movement. It was moving at ten to twelve knots and overtook me. I must have had it in my vision for about twenty minutes.'

On 27 August, Bramwell Holmes, of Penryn, and his wife and son, were in their motorboat, off Restronguet Point, when they noticed a disturbance in the water and two large, mottled grey humps broke the surface, each about five feet across and two feet high. The Holmes family observed the monster for about ten minutes and glimpsed a snake-like head just before it submerged.

A few days later, from Gyllyngvase Beach, Donald Ferris, of Falmouth, saw a creature like a gigantic eel, fifty or sixty feet in length, with a humped back.

Then a Morgawr was seen ashore, on the morning of 12

Ernst's Nightjarman is invoked for Leonora Carrington.
[Max Ernst, *La dame Ovale*, 1939.]

September, when two holidaymakers, Allan and Sally White from Gloucestershire, saw a brown 'something', fifteen to twenty feet long, slide into the water from Grebe Beach. Like so many other witnesses, they had 'never seen anything like it before'.

There were dozens of Morgawr sightings that summer, which seemed to indicate that the unusually hot weather conditions were ideal for monster hunting. It probably simply meant that there were more people spending more time by or in the sea than would have been the case had the summer been less of a scorcher. I went swimming almost every day, and kept an eye open for Morgawr, but I did not see the contrary critter again until summer was well and truly over.

David Clarke, editor of *Cornish Life* magazine, was planning a feature on Cornwall's famous monster, and he intended to make some jocular references to my role in the story. On the morning of 17 November, he took me down to Parson's Beach for a photo-session. I was supposed to stand on the rocks, making suitably theatrical invocational gestures, while David snapped away with his Pentax. I carried two 'props': my wizardry stick and my aged Rollei, which was loaded with colour negative film. As things turned out, David Clarke soon stopped joking about Morgawr.

After I had done my bit, playing the eccentric shaman, I suddenly noticed a dark, double-humped, shape break the surface of the water, about two hundred yards distant. Then a small head on a long neck rose up, the body submerging as the animal swam powerfully back and forth. It was Morgawr, large as life and clear as day. I pointed it out to the sceptical Mr Clarke. He later wrote:

> Doc drew my attention to an object halfway across the river - a small dark head poking out of the water. We both stood on large rocks for a better view and I attached a telephoto lens to my camera. The object slowly moved nearer and I could see that it was definitely a head, probably a seal. It came within seventy or eighty feet and started to move very slowly up and down river in a zig-zag pattern. It was only when I saw it side-on that I observed that the greenish-black head was supported on a long arched neck, more slender than that of a seal. In the wave troughs at least four or five feet of the neck were visible. There was a slow movement of water stretching back behind the head and neck for about ten feet, and at one point a gently-rounded shiny black body broke the surface.

The creature's ugly head carried a pair of stumpy little horns, and looked like the head of a gigantic snail. I noticed a pale mouth, but the animal appeared to have no eyes, unless, like a snail's, they were on retractile stalks. I reckoned the animal was about fifteen to eighteen feet long, smooth skinned, dark green in colour. I photographed it several times [see opposite], as did David, before his dog began to bark. The sudden noise seemed to startle our

1: Doc Shiels, Falmouth, 1978. [ANS / FPL]

2A: Wizard of the Western World.

2B: Raising daughter Kate. [Lawrence Lawry]

3A: Busking in Padstow...   **3B**: ... and Killarney.

4: Gareth and Chris Shiels with the Punch and Judy Show, 1975.
[Ander Gunn]

5: 'Distant Humps', 1977. The cast with Chris Fairbank.

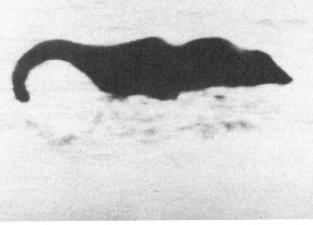

6 A&B: Morgawr, the Great Cornish Sea Serpent, photographed by 'Mary F', February 1976. [ANS / FPL]

7 A&B: Triple exposure of Doc and Morgawr, by David Clarke, November 17, 1976, ... and detail. [David Clarke]

8A: Witches on Parson's Beach, below Mawnan Old Church, Midsummer 1976. [ANS / FPL]

8B: BBC TV crew hunting Mogawr in Falmouth Bay, November 1980. [ANS / FPL]

9 A&B: Morag, the monster of Loch Morar, photographed by Miss M. Lindsay, January 31, 1977. [FPL]

10A: Pengersick Castle.

10B: Mawnan Old Church. [Janet & Colin Bord]

11A: Witchcraft in Mawnan Woods. [ANS / FPL]

11B: Invoking Owlman. [ANS / FPL]

12A: David Hoy.

12B: Max Maven.

12C: Prof. Michael McCormick.

12D: Masklyn.

13A: Charles Fort. [FPL] **13B**: Max Ernst.

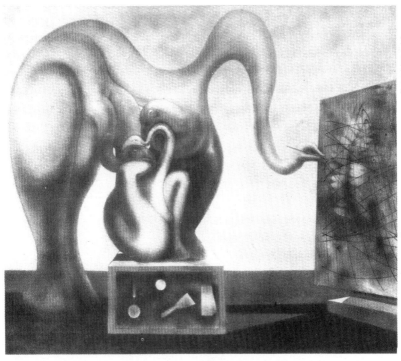

13C: 'Surrealism and Painting' (1942) by Max Ernst.

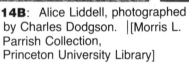

14B: Alice Liddell, photographed by Charles Dodgson. |[Morris L. Parrish Collection, Princeton University Library]

14A: Charles Lutwidge Dodgson, a.k.a. Lewis Carroll. [Gernsheim Collection, University of Texas, Austin]

14C: Cornish fairies? 1975/76?

15A: Francis Griffiths and Elsie Wright with Geoffrey Hodson in Cottingley Glen, 1921. [Brotherton Collection, Leeds]

15B: Elsie and a fairy friend, Cottingley, 1917. [FPL]

16A: The Loch Ness Monster, photographed by Hugh Gray, November 1933. [FPL]

16B: Doc in the ruined tower of Urquhart Castle overlooking Loch Ness, May 21, 1977. [ANS / FPL]

17 A-C: Nessie. A full frame (top) of the famous number one photograph by Doc Shiels, May 21, 1977, with an enlargement (left – see also back cover), and (right) an enlargement of the second shot. [ANS / FPL]

18A: Tim Dinsdale monster hunting in his boat 'Water Horse' below Urquhart Castle. [FPL]

18B: The Goodyear airship 'Europa' over Urquhart Castle with monster hunters on board, June 1982. Also in sight is Adrian Shine's Loch Ness Project research barge. [Ivor Newby / FPL]

19A: Nessie, photographed from a spot near Achnahannet by an anonymous woman on a cycling holiday, September 1983. [FPL]

19B: Holmes and Watson encounter the Loch Ness Monster. A scene from *The Private Life of Sherlock Holmes* (1970). [Associated Press]

20: G(reat)-U(nknown)-IN-NESS. [Poster for Guinness].

21A: Doc and three witches at Lough Leane, Killarney, Co.Kerry, August 1981. [ANS / FPL]

21B: 'Ted' Holiday (right) with Lionel Leslie and Holly Arnold, attempting to net a *peiste* at Lough Auna, Connemara, Co.Galway, 1968.

22A: The 'Great Wurrum' of Lough Leane, photographed by Pat Kelly, August 1981. [FPL]

22B: 'Worm Stones' by the Cliffs of Moher, Co.Clare. [ANS / FPL]

23A: 'Moby Mick', Keel Lough, Achill Island, Co.Mayo, September 1983. [ANS / FPL]

23B: A marine *peiste*, Liscannor Bay, September 1983. [ANS / FPL]

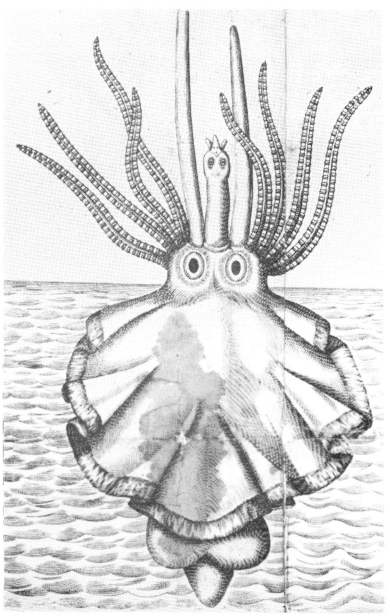

24 *Dinoteuthis proboscideus*... the Dingle Squid, driven ashore in October 1673.

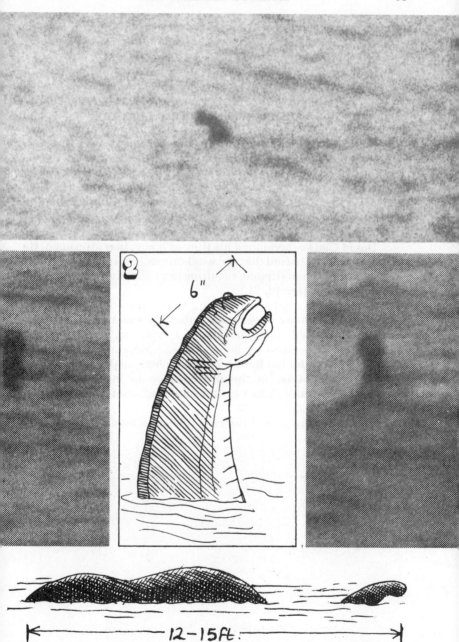

Morgawr; details from a sequence photographed by Doc Shiels, November 17, 1976, with a sketch of its appearance for most of the sighting. [ANS / FPL]

monster, which vanished in a swirl of water. We waited for an hour or more in case the Morgawr returned, but it didn't, so we went for a well-deserved drink.

In the pub at Mawnan Smith, David and I drew sketches of the thing we had seen. I wanted to be sure that we had both observed the creature in, roughly, the same way. David had obviously been quite shaken by the experience, and I, to say the least, had not really expected such a phenomenal sighting. The timing was so perfect, the animal seemed to have surfaced as a direct result of my shamanic antics. This fact alone made David suspicious. 'Bloody wizard,' he said, 'how the hell did you do it?' A tricky question, to which I had no ready answer. He had, in the past, seen me working as a stage magician, so David's incredulity was quite understandable. The raising of Morgawr was a spectacular feat of conjuring, but the conjurer was almost as puzzled as his audience.

David Clarke developed his film, at home, that afternoon. He was disappointed to find that the wind-on mechanism of his, usually reliable, camera had slipped, resulting in a collection of double and triple exposures [see pl. 7].

Later, he accused me of 'doing a Uri Geller' on his Pentax, but I knew he was simply experiencing the jinx which often bedevils would-be monster photographers. I was luckier, and my photographs, processed by Boots, showed Morgawr in mid-river. Unfortunately, I did not have a telephoto lens, so the pictures lack detail. All the same, in the presence of an independent and 'respectable' witness, I had at last captured a serpent-dragon on film. I was thrilled.

The following year, I raised a few more monsters.

5

MONSTERMIND

'Harrangue the waves.'
André Breton and Philippe Soupault

1977 was a psi-power-packed year. A year in which sea-changes were suffered by things and ourselves, richly and strangely.

I had, for some time, been in regular contact with a number of professional psychics, and early in 1977 seven of us formed a dragon-raising team which we called the Psychic Seven International, or P-S-I. Our intention was to, collectively, attempt the invocation of aquatic serpent-dragons throughout the world. That first experiment, dubbed 'Monstermind' by the *Daily Mirror*, commenced on the last day of January, Imbolc or Brigid's Eve, and lasted three days. It was spectacularly successful, and, during the period of our experiment, monsters were seen in the USA, USSR, and Britain.

A large 'saurian' was reported in San Francisco Bay, and 'Champ' reared up in Lake Champlain, Vermont and New York State. A serpent-dragon, forty feet long, was seen in Lake Kok-kol, Soviet Central Asia. On 31 January, two photographs of 'Morag', the beastie of Loch Morar, were taken by Miss M. Lindsay of Musselburgh [see pl. 9]. On the same day, John Smith saw 'Shiela' of Loch Shiel. At least three sightings of Nessie were reported, by Mr Fleming and his daughter Helen, Mr and Mrs Alex McLeod, and by Pat Scott-Innes. Our success at Loch Ness was largely due to the on-the-spot presence of Pat, one of the seven. She has the right initials in her name. Gerald Bennett, who had seen Morgawr previously in 1975, took three colour photographs of the Cornish monster from Parson's Beach. On February 1st, Ray Hopley saw Morgawr off Trefusis Point.

Around midnight, on the final night of the experiment, I telephoned team-member Dr David Hoy [see pl. 12a], in Paducah, Kentucky, USA. Our conversation, discussing the invocations, was broadcast live to American radio listeners and, the following day, an edited recording went out on BBC's 'Newsbeat' programme. David Hoy was at that time America's top psychic. A larger-than-life character, he relished his role as the 'Grand Panjandrum of Extra Sensory Perception'. Within weeks of his valued participation in 'Monstermind', David suffered a massive heart attack.

Another 'Monstermind' team-member, Major Leslie May MBE, of Edinburgh, became ill after taking part in the experiment. Since 1977, I have not received a word of news from, or concerning, our colleagues in India, Mexico and the USSR. It appears that five members of the original P-S-I group succumbed to 'psychic backlash'. Can dragon-raising seriously damage our health, or do we put it down to coincidence? I think it all has to do with the fact that, one way or another, we have to pay for what we get. Our success was costly. Tim Dinsdale had, several times, advised me to watch out for the nasty 'side effects' of monster hunting. My family and I were beset with sicknesses and irritations for a while (I had an unpleasant attack of shingles), but fought back with the surrealist shaman's greatest weapon: humour. Ribald guffaws will exorcise most negative spirits, but the corny old cliche still applies: there is no good without evil, no evil without good.

I warily prepared for phase two of the 'Monstermind' experiment, and recruited some new P-S-I members. Beginning at Beltane, we planned to continue the invocations for three months, up to Lugnasad, and to concentrate our efforts on the Loch Ness Monster.

Ness is a significant word which may be derived from the Old Norse, *nes*, meaning nose, or from the ancient Indo-European root *ned*, to wet or flood. There is an island, Nesis, now called Nisita, in the Bay of Naples. Nessus was the river-swimming centaur whose poisonous blood killed the monster-killing Herakles. Remember these things.

Loch Ness, twenty two miles long, up to one and a half miles wide, over seven hundred feet deep, is the largest freshwater lake in the British Isles. It fills much of the north-eastern end of the Great Glen, from Fort Augustus almost all the way to Inverness. A dramatic and atmospheric setting, the home of the world's most famous monster.

It, the 'thing', was first mentioned in Adamnan's *Vita Sancti Columbae*, which describes the Irish saint's encounter with a 'water beast' in the River Ness. Columba was, at that time - about fourteen centuries ago - busy converting pagan Northern Picts in the kingdom of Brude mac Maelchon. One of Brude's men, Lugne Mocumin, had been ordered by the holy Columba to swim over the water and fetch a ferry coble, moored at the opposite bank. Lugne dived into the river, then up came the monster 'and with great roaring rushed towards the man swimming in the middle of the stream'. Columba raised his staff and his voice, commanding the beast to 'go back with all speed'. The poor terrified monster did as it was told, 'more quickly than if it had been pulled back with ropes'.

Such hagiographic stories should be taken with a pinch of sea-salt, but this tale contains some interesting cryptozoological clues.

Another 'Great Beast' lived in the Great Glen for a while.

Boleskine House, north of Foyers, was the home of Aleister Crowley during the first decade of this century. The infamous magician experimented with the Abramelin Ritual at Boleskine, and succeeded in conjuring up strange 'shadowy shapes' which are said to have haunted the area for years. Crowley may have even invoked the serpent-dragon. He had a lot of tricks up his sleeve. I have more to say about Frater Perdurabo, Laird of Boleskine, later.

Local people had, for centuries, known about the monster, only they tended to refer to it as a kelpie, *Each Uisge*, or water-horse, a kind of aquatic bogey-beast. Scores of Highland lochs and rivers are connected with these supernatural shape-shifters, and it was not until 1933 that Loch Ness became generally known as *the* place where Scotland's biggest beastie could be seen. This was the year that Alex Campbell presented Nessie to the press. Campbell was the loch's water bailiff, employed by the Ness Fisheries Board, and Fort Augustus correspondent for the *Inverness Courier* and the *Northern Chronicle*. On 2 and 3 May, the two newspapers published reports, received from Alex Campbell, concerning the experience of a local couple who had seen an enormous creature churning up the waters of the loch 'like a simmering cauldron', before vanishing 'in a boiling mass of foam'. During the following months, more monster reports were published in the *Courier*, including a letter from a London businessman, Mr George Spicer, who, while driving with his wife between Dores and Foyers, had encountered something like 'a dragon or prehistoric animal' actually crossing the road some fifty yards ahead [see below]. The creature 'seemed to have a long neck which moved up and down in the manner of a scenic railway'.

Towards the autumn of 1933, the Loch Ness Monster - already nicknamed 'Nessie' - was internationally known as the ultimate, journalistic, 'silly season' gimmick. I do not have to remind Fortean readers of this state of affairs. It is the way of the newspaper world. The story has been well documented, time and time again. But...

Georrge Spicer's drawing of the thing he saw on the road to Foyers.

But we should consider a couple of things:

The *silly season* is, usually, confined to the hot summer months. Nessie was active during those months, but the national media didn't really join in the game until the Ray Bradburying October time.

1933 was the longest, hottest summer on record, before 1976.

Etymologically, 'silly', usually accepted as meaning frivolously foolish, originally stems from the Old English *saelig*, related to the Gothic *sels*, meaning happy and/or good. 'Season', from the Old French *seson*, from Latin *satio*, means time to sow. So... the 'silly season' is a good time. 'Gimmick' was, originally, a magicians' word. It is something that makes tricks work. Make of this what I do, if you will.

October is heavily associated with what is popularly known as Hallowe'en. The Rev. Murdo Campbell of Fort Augustus seems to have been aware of this when he announced at that time (the Sabbath being the 30th) 'that the word "monster" is really not applicable to the Loch Ness animal but it is truly applicable to those who deliberately sin against the light of law and revelation.' I will not mention this 'Wee Free' minister again, but note his surname.

On Sunday, 13 November 1933, after church, Mr Hugh Gray snapped the first known photograph of the Loch Ness Monster. It was, in his words, 'an object of considerable dimensions'. Personally, I regard this photograph as one of the best ever taken of the creature. It is so convincingly *weird*.

Nessie continued to be seen, by thousands of people, throughout the nineteen thirties and beyond. I do not intend to repeat, here, what has appeared in so many publications. Look elsewhere for details of the Loch Ness saga. As far as this convoluted narrative is concerned, we had better get back to the 'Monstermind' experiment, 1977.

After getting our act together on May Day, at Padstow, Chris and I, with a couple of friends, headed up to the Highlands by train.

On the evening of 20 May, at Loch Ness, we did secret surrealist things, involving Guinness, an occult sigil, and some cold peaty water.

At about half past eight on the beautiful Saturday morning of 21 May, Chris and I were standing in the car park of our hotel, the Inchnacardoch Lodge, with four other people (our friends, Richard and Lynn Smith from Carharrack, and a young couple from Bolton), enjoying the view of a mirror-smooth Loch Ness, chatting as we waited to be summoned into the dining room for breakfast. Suddenly, Chris called our attention to three dark, smoothly-rounded humps, gliding through the water in the direction of Fort Augustus. Nessie! All six of us saw it, or *them*. It could have been a trio of Nessies, about three hundred yards away. Everyone experienced a thrill of excitement at the uncanny, awesome spectacle. Not one of us had a camera to hand. Mine, a new 35mm SLR loaded with film and fitted with a telephoto lens, was upstairs in the hotel bedroom. For a moment, I considered dashing indoors to fetch it, then the two leading humps slipped under the surface, followed quickly by the third, leaving hardly a ripple. My emotions were a mixture of elation and frustration. The sighting only lasted a few seconds, but it was real. Now I *knew* for sure that the monster existed, and I was pretty certain that I would see it again that day. I vowed to have my camera ready for action, at all times, during our stay at Loch Ness.

After breakfast, Chris and I decided to walk along the A82 as far as Invermoriston, keeping a fairly constant sharp eye to starboard for any signs of the serpent-dragon. It was a warm sunny day, and the stroll helped to build up a healthy thirst. Some pints of Guinness were consumed at Invermoriston, and we had a conversation with a local melodian-player. Then, setting off in the direction of Drumnadrochit, we stuck our thumbs out, hoping to hitch a ride. After no more than five or ten minutes, a friendly young man stopped and offered us a lift. He was on his way to Inverness to deliver some motor parts, and drove at quite frightening speed, ignoring all the roadside warnings about wandering sheep, depositing us at Drumnadrochit in no time. Waving farewell to our chauffeur, we decided to settle our nerves with a wee dram at the hotel. Being rather partial to those Highland single malts, I confess to drinking more than just a single (booze is again mentioned because so many people equate visions of Nessie with visions of pink elephants... that's right, pink *elephants*).

Squiffily, we set off to do some monster hunting.

Urquhart Castle, or Castle Urquhart, depending on the way words are shuffled, is a twelfth century ruin built on the site of a Celtic fort which, in turn, was built on the site of the sixth century (and, of course, vitrified) *munitio* of King Brude mac Maelchon. There is treasure still hidden there, according to the guidebooks. More interestingly, a 'plague' or 'pestilence' is said to have been operculated, 'miraculously', deep below the place.

As Chris and I came down the road from Lewiston, approaching the castle, we noticed some strange wakes in Urquhart Bay, where there have been more sightings of the monster than in any other part of Loch Ness. We explored the castle that afternoon.

Around four o'clock, while Chris was in the castle grounds, I nosed around the ruined tower and found a window, overlooking the loch, which seemed to provide a good vantage point for a Nessie spotter [see pl. 16b]. Quite suddenly, a small dark head on the end of a long sinuous neck broke the surface of the water, about a hundred yards away. It was, undoubtedly, the Loch Ness Monster, proudly erectile, ready to be snapped. I instantly raised my camera and shot two pictures during the few seconds that the creature was visible [see pl. 17]. Its neck was about four or five feet long, greenish brown with a yellowish underside, smooth and glossy. Its open-mouthed head was tiny in relation to the muscular neck. The animal turned away from me, straightening its neck before sinking vertically.

I stood there mesmerized by the brief dreamlike vision. My heart beating rapidly, hands shaking as I lowered the camera, whispering expletives, ecstatic.

After a few minutes, I calmed myself sufficiently to go and find Chris, who was sitting on the grass enjoying the fine weather. I gave her my news. Chris grinned. 'I knew it,' she said.

For the next few days (including my birthday), we kept watch on the loch, but with little hope of witnessing Nessie again. Already I had been much luckier than most would-be monster spotters, now I was anxious to get back to Cornwall and have that important roll of film developed. Chris shared my sentiments, so we left Loch Ness, spent a night at Spean Bridge, then caught a train homewards.

Rattling down the old West Highland line, towards Glasgow, I sat puffing at my pipe and thinking about the incredible events of the previous Saturday. Incredible was the word. Would anyone believe me? What if the photographs were duds and didn't show a thing? I wondered if anyone else had seen the monster when it came up to be photographed. Maybe someone somewhere shot movie footage of the beast that afternoon. As it happens, some weeks later, a reporter told me that a man, calling himself Roy Benson, had telephoned the Aberdeen *Press & Journal* on the afternoon of May 21st, claiming to have just seen Nessie in Urquhart Bay.

As the train from Glasgow rolled into Redruth station, we saw David Clarke waiting on the platform, eager for information. I had telephoned him earlier, asking him to meet us. We had hardly stepped down from the coach before he began to bombard us with questions. 'Unless the Loch Ness hoodoo has hit us,' I said, handing him the film, 'the answer to your biggest question is on there.'

David arranged for the High Speed Ektachrome film to be processed by Newquay Colour Services, the laboratory which handles most of the colour transparency work for *Cornish Life*. A couple of days later, after he had carefully examined each slide, projecting them onto a large screen, David telephoned me, clearly excited. 'You seem to have done it,' he said. 'Two beautiful photographs of the ugly thing. Get round here at once!'

Within the hour, I was sitting in a darkened room at the *Cornish Life* office, viewing the results of our Nessie hunt. Teasingly, David built up the tension by projecting ten pictures which preceded my monster shots. They were typical 'holiday snaps', landscape 'views' and such. Then came number eleven. In the lower centre of an expanse of blue water was the image of the beast itself. [see pl. 17a] It simply had to be the clearest photograph ever taken of the world's favourite monster, just as I had seen it through my viewfinder. There was the gently curving, muscular neck, greenish brown, with its pale band down the front. There was the small blunt head, light reflecting off its glossy skin, and the menacing open mouth. There... was Nessie. The next slide [see pl. 17c], my second shot of the creature, showed it turning away, moving to the right of the frame, straightening its neck as it prepared to submerge.

'Amazing,' said Dave, in a respectfully hushed tone.

'We certainly seem to have cracked it,' I admitted. 'I was scared to death that the bloody pictures would be fogged, or blank, or lost in the lab. It happens all the time with photographs of monsters.'

David nodded, recalling his experience with Morgawr, and his jinxed Pentax.

During the next few days, I announced the good news to fellow members of the 'Monstermind' crew, and to interested parties such as Bob Rickard, Rip Hepple and Tim Dinsdale. Then I decided to tell the press. My best approach seemed to be to contact Mike Truscott, a Falmouth journalist who had written several stories about Morgawr. I went to see Mike, taking the slides with me, and he was duly impressed. He telephoned the Glasgow *Daily Record*, the newspaper which had published that very first photograph of Nessie, back in 1933. Their picture editor, Martin Gilfeather, asked for both slides to be rushed to him, immediately, by fast train. Prudently, I agreed to send one only. Very soon, my first shot was speeding its way back up to Scotland.

The following day, Gilfeather telephoned asking for 'before and after' shots, those 'holiday snaps', from the same strip of film, to establish the fact that I was actually at Loch Ness when I said I was. A selection was duly dispatched, the *Daily Record* carefully examined them all, matching up edge-numbers, and so on. They also contacted the Inchnacardoch Lodge Hotel, to check that Chris and I had really stayed there. By this time, the *Record*'s national big sister paper, the *Daily Mirror*, was in on the act, and a series of interviews began. The reporters seemed amused by my claim to have raised the monster by 'psychic' means, and the *Mirror* decided to link its story with the Queen's Silver Jubilee celebrations. Finally, on Thursday 9 June, Nessie made the front pages of both newspapers.

The *Daily Record* printed the picture in full colour, while the *Daily Mirror*'s headline yelled: *UP FOR THE JUBILEE NESSIE*!

Then I tried to get my photographs returned. The *Record* was holding a unique original, there were no copy slides of the Nessie shots. The newspaper promised to send all my pictures back at once, but it was almost two nail-biting weeks before I received the monster slide. My 'holiday snaps' had been 'temporarily misplaced'. I haven't seen them since. Tim Dinsdale had warned me about this kind of thing.

A Falmouth photo-journalist, David Benchley, made a glass copy-negative of the second Nessie shot. The original was airmailed to a member of the 'Monstermind' team, the American psychic Max Maven [see pl. 12b]. Its carefully sealed package duly arrived in Boston, Massachusetts, but the photograph had vanished! Things were beginning to go wrong. The famous Loch Ness hoodoo had started to take effect.

BRITAIN'S BIGGEST DAILY SALE   7p   Thursday, June 9, 1977

Up for the Jubilee
NESSIE !

NESSIE has surfaced again — By Appointment.
   She'd planned it all along, of course. There was no need for fancy gadgets to lure her from the deep. Not this year.
   All it needed was . . . the Jubilee.
   And the Beastie from Loch Ness popped up, right on cue, for a peek at the celebrations.
   Nessie's Command Performance was captured in this believe-it-or-not photograph, right, by monster-watcher "Doctor" Tony Shiels from Falmouth, Cornwall. The "Doc" — he bought a doctorate in the States for five dollars — reckons Nessie was 100 yards away when he took the picture. And he brought Nessie to the surface, he claims, by using telepathy.
   Nessie might argue with that. She's just as likely to have risen for a Jubilee knees-up.

'964, let's see more.   ON time for '69.   STILL alive in '75.   MORE tricks in '76.

Nessie through the Looking Glass.

Another journalist, Frank Durham, made copy slides of the number one picture. The day I received these, the glass negative of number two was dropped and smashed. My instincts told me to abandon the 'Monstermind' experiment. I was obviously pushing my luck too far, and suffering a kind of 'backlash' effect as a consequence. So, on the seventh day of the seventh month of nineteen seventy seven, I dropped out of the team.

Enlarged colour copies of my first Nessie picture were, by now, circulating around the world, getting published here and there, receiving both damnation and admiration in roughly equal doses. One of these copies was submitted to Ground Saucer Watch (GSW) in Phoenix, Arizona, for computer analysis. The saucer-men opined that either the creature was translucent or the photograph was a double exposure. Obviously they regarded me as a hoaxer. My reputation as a magician tended to encourage other people to think along similar lines. I received some nasty letters. On the positive side, the photographs, now designated ANS.1 and ANS.2, were enthusiastically supported by Bob Rickard, Janet and Colin Bord, and Tim Dinsdale. I eventually sent the original ANS.1, by registered mail, to Tim. When he told me that it had arrived safely, I heaved a sigh of relief.

A week after Tim received ANS.1, a bomb went off in the Ridge Theatre, San Francisco, where Luis Būnuel's surrealist movie, *That Obscure Object of Desire*, was being shown. For some reason, when I heard about the incident, it seemed ominous.

One day, Ken Campbell arrived in Ponsanooth and said he wanted to produce a show, destined for a London theatre, all about the Shiels family and our monster-raising adventures. We decided to call it *Distant Humps* [see pl. 5]. Predictively, my script included the line: 'Guinness, a work of black art, there's genius in it.' After just three, well received, try-out, public performances in Falmouth, things went wrong. We scrapped the show.

Straight after Samhain, and a play called *Spooks* (Count Dracula v Sherlock Holmes), I swore an affidavit [see following page] declaring that my Loch Ness photographs were genuine. This document was sent to Tim Dinsdale, who then submitted my original ANS.1 slide to the eminent photographic scientist Dr Vernon Harrison (until 1976 President of the Royal Photographic Society) for examination. On 3 December, Dr Harrison returned the picture with his analysis, in the form of a letter. I reproduce the affidavit with just one comment: it was the solicitor, or his secretary, who didn't know how to spell 'Ektachrome'. Dr Harrison's letter is also reproduced [over] and I think it is utterly fair. Various writers have interpreted his comments in amusingly contradictory ways, selectively quoting whichever parts would

Continued on p80 ☞

I <u>ANTHONY NICOL SHIELS</u> of 3 Vale View Ponsanooth Truro in the County of

Cornwall <u>DO SOLEMNLY AND SINCERELY DECLARE</u> as follows:-

1.   On Saturday May Twenty first One thousand nine hundred and seventy

seven I was exploring the ruins of Castle Urquhart on the shores of Loch Ness

in Scotland when at approximately 4 p.m. in the waters of the Loch below the

Castle I saw what I believed to be a large aquatic creature.   Its head and

neck stood above the surface about four or five feet in length.   Its colour

was greenish brown with a paler underside.

2.   I watched the creature through the view finder of my camera which was

fitted with a telephoto lens and it turned away from me and straightened its

muscular neck before sinking straight down very smoothly.   I managed to take

two photographs in the five or six seconds before the creature submerged.

The two photographs are now produced and shown to me and marked "ANS 1" and

"ANS 2".

3.   My camera was a 35mm SLR Zenith EM fitted with a 135 mm Chinon telephoto

lens.   The film used was a high speed Ektocrome.

4.   I believe that the photographs show one of the creatures known as "The

Loch Ness Monsters" and I wish to declare that the two aforementioned

photographs are genuine.

<u>AND</u> I make this solemn declaration conscientiously believing the same to be

true and by virtue of the provisions of the Statutory Declarations Act 1835.

<u>DECLARED</u> at Falmouth this   )
)
Fourteenth   )
)
day of   November   1977   )   *H. N. Shiel*

                             Before me,

                                                  Stephen Flood

                             A Solicitor   (S.T.H. HOSKING)

My affidavit.

From V. G. W. Harrison
Ph.D., F.Inst.P., F.R.P.S., F.Illum.Eng.S.

Dear Mr. Dinsdale,

I have examined the photographic transparency stated to
have been taken by Mr. A.N. Shiels on Saturday 21 May 1977 from
the shore of Loch Ness in the vicinity of Castle Urquhart.
This examination has been made through a binocular microscope at
all magnifications up to ×100.   I find the transparency to be
quite normal and there is no evidence of double exposure,
superimposition of images or handwork with bleach or dye.

The object depicted is certainly not a branch of a tree,
a trick of the light or an effect of uneven processing.   Under
magnification a small reptilian head is seen looking towards a
point on the right of the photographer.   The lighting comes
from behind, and somewhat to the right of, the photographer;
and the foreshortening of the water shows that the object was
photographed from a considerable distance through a long focus
lens.   The creature has a wide mouth, partly open, and light is
reflected strongly from the lower lip, which is presumably wet.
There is an indication of two eyes and a stubby nose.   The head
is attached to a long neck whose girth increases as it approaches
the water.   The neck is smooth and reflects light strongly,
and it appears to be paler in colour on its lower side.   The
course of the neck can be traced for some inches below the
surface of the water until it is lost to view because of the
turbidity of the water.   The image of the submerged part is
distorted by the surface wavelets of the water, and I find these
distortions to be entirely naturalistic.   There is even a
wavelet that has been reflected back from the left side of the
neck and caught the light of the sun.

It is not possible to say from a single still transparency
exactly what the photograph represents.   The obvious explanation
is that the photograph depicts a living creature strongly
resembling a Plesiosaurus.   However, it could be a hoax.   For
example, a diver might have made a model of the head and neck
and be holding it above the water while he himself was submerged.
A third possibility is that the photograph is not of an outdoor
scene at all, but is a reduction of an imaginative painting
executed by a competent artist.   To produce a sufficiently
deceptive painting would require skill and a detailed knowledge
of the effects of light reflected from, and transmitted through,
rippled water;   and it is just these effects which I find so
impressive in the photograph.

While I feel that the alternative explanations I have
suggested are not very plausible, they can only be excluded by
a study of any independent evidence that may be available.

Yours sincerely,

V. G. W. Harrison

Dr Vernon Harrison's letter to Tim Dinsdale.

seem to support their arguments, pro and con.

Sir Peter Scott telegraphed me, asking if he could use ANS.1 in a series of lectures he was presenting in Antarctica. Permission was, of course, granted, and *Nessiteras* flew south.

1977 went out with a bang, as a series of mysterious and still unexplained explosions shook Cornwall.

The first weeks of 1978 were taken up with the writing and rehearsing of a new play, *The Gallavant Variations*, for our company. We opened in Falmouth, at the Arts Theatre, to a full house, and received some good press reviews. But then the *Sun* heard a whisper that our show was just a wee bit shocking. We soon hit the headlines again: THE WEIRDEST FAMILY IN THE LAND! *Gallavant* did not last very long. Financial support was withdrawn and we were forced back on the streets to try and raise a few pounds by busking. Soon we were banned from almost every 'respectable' holiday town in Cornwall. I began to feel a trifle paranoid.

At the tail end of April, Janet and Colin Bord came down to Cornwall, collecting material for their splendid book, *Alien Animals*. They took a close look at the woods around Mawnan Old Church, Parson's Beach, Falmouth Bay, and at the Padstow Obbyoss. Our gang was at Padstow too, of course [see pl. 3a], on May Day, hoping to build up our shamanic muscles for another series of invocational experiments.

I desperately wanted to see and, hopefully, photograph the Owlman. Also, I decided to try and raise the odd Pisky, Bucca or Spriggan. In these provocative endeavours, I was assisted by my daughters, Kate and Meig [see pl. 11]. On and off, between Beltaine and Samhain, we did our stuff.

Early in June, 16-year-old Miss Opie, from Camborne, saw 'a monster like a devil flying up through the trees near Old Mawnan Church'. Owlman was back, but we missed his performance. However, we noticed some unusual coloured lights in the sky over Falmouth Bay. They probably signified nothing at all. I had a weird dream about the Owlman (and Max Ernst), in which Owlman turned into Nightjarman [see p63]. The following year, I wrote a trilogy of plays about the *Caprimulgiformes*, but I digress.

Peter Redgrove, the poet and novelist, told me he had seen a 'shimmering pisky', somewhere near Falmouth. Peter sees all manner of things, or so he says. I suspect him of being a bit of a Jungian.

David Hoy, recovering from his illness, bravely offered to augment our psi-power by projecting Owlman-raising thoughts from Kentucky to Cornwall. Then he had another heart attack. Too much fried chicken, mayhap? Or was it psychic backlash?

I suffered backlash in the middle of a fire-spitting routine when the wind suddenly changed and my fuel-soaked whiskers exploded into flame. Meig was banjaxed by stabbing abdominal pains and sickness. Kate was thrown by a usually docile horse, breaking her arm. These, and a devil's dozen of other unpleasant things, all happened to the family in July and August.

On 2 August, three French girls, on holiday, saw Owlman near Mawnan Old Church. One of them described the thing as being like 'a great big furry bird with a gaping mouth and big round eyes'. The Shiels family was too busy having a bad time to be at Mawnan when the winged weirdo turned up. My son Ewan was hurt when he was knocked down by a hit-and-run motorcyclist. The biker and his bike were all decked out in black. Two of our feline familiars suddenly died of a mystery illness. The vet admitted bafflement. Then Tom Fool's Theatre disbanded. There was something thumb-prickingly nasty in the air, to be sure. It was getting me down.

After Hallowe'en, I called a halt to the invocational activities for a while and concentrated on other, different and quite marvellous, pursuits. The year turned, 1978 was behind us. By the spring of 1979, I felt ready to face dragons again...

Irish dragons.

6

CELTIC CONNECTIONS

*'We are the music-makers
And we are the dreamers of dreams.'*
Arthur O'Shaughnessy

IRELAND has a long tradition of serpent-dragons. Patrick Kennedy, in his *Legendary Fictions of the Irish Celts*, says: 'We have more than one pool deriving its name from having been infested by a worm or serpent of the days of the heroes. Fion M'Cumhaill killed several of these.'

By the fifth century, St Patrick was said to have banished all remaining serpents from the land, but that Romanized Brit bishop's powers have been greatly overrated.

The *Book of Lismore* tells of St Seonan's encounter with the 'repulsive, outlandish, fierce, and very terrifying' Monster of Scattery Island, off the Clare coast. St Coemgen subdued a serpent which dwelt in the Upper Lake at Glendalough, Co. Wicklow. The seventh century St Mo-Chua of Balla, Co. Mayo, put a Connaght dragon in its place. But, in spite of all this saintly dragon-bashing, Christianity could not rid Ireland of its repulsive *peiste*.

An Irish Gaelic word, *peiste*, sometimes written *piast* or *paystha*, means worm. The Ollpiast is a 'great wurrum' or serpent. *Peiste* can also mean pest or pestilence, and derives from the Latin *pestis*. It sounds very like the Scottish Gaelic *beiste*, beast, and the Highland Loch na Beiste is as serpent-infested as Lough na Peiste in Co. Wexford. There is an area on the Kerry coast known as Imleach Peiste, meaning the field or place of the worm-pestilence. To *peste* is to utter a curse or imprecation.

I have spent a lot of time in Ireland. It is the land of my paternal ancestors, the O Siadhails, and I feel at home there. Year after year, I have travelled the country, appearing at fairs, in pubs, and on the streets, playing music and performing feats of legerdemain. Just after May Day 1979, I found myself in Co. Kerry, and decided to attempt the conjuration of some 'wurrums'.

I concentrated my efforts on Lough Leane, near Killarney. This beautiful lake is said to be haunted by the great warrior-wizard, O'Donoghue, whose treasure is guarded by a triple-headed monster. My invocations were unsuccessful (success isn't everything), the worm refused to turn up, but a weird atmosphere in the area indicated some kind of paranormal presence. I vowed to return and try again one day.

Irish lake monsters have been regularly seen and reported throughout the present century, especially in Co. Kerry and the Connemara region of Co. Galway. 'Ted' Holiday [see pl. 21b], Peter

Costello, and Graham McEwan have carefully documented some of the most interesting sightings. I recommend their books to anyone interested in the problem of the peiste... and it *is* a problem. There is something disturbingly odd, uncanny and puzzling about many of the lakes in which these creatures are encountered: they seem to be far too small to support their monstrous inhabitants.

Lough Bran, in Co. Kerry, is only about five hundred yards long, yet it is reported to contain a bizarre animal, 'black as soot', resembling a cross between 'a giant seal and a dragon'. The Lough Bran monster has been reported by a number of witnesses. It was seen by two brothers, local farmers, during the summer of 1979, shortly after I had been trying to raise the serpent of Lough Leane, just fifteen miles away.

Lackagh Lake, five miles from Killarney, is several times smaller than Lough Bran, but a long-necked creature with stumpy horns has been seen there in recent years.

The wild bogland of Connemara is riddled with lakes, most of them small and shallow. Nevertheless, monsters appear in them, frightening the anglers who are attracted to the area. Lough Fadda is about one and a half miles long and six hundred yards across at its widest point. On a June evening in 1954, Georgina Carberry, a Clifden librarian and an experienced angler, was fishing from a boat on the lough, accompanied by three friends. After hooking several trout, the anglers decided to pull ashore and have some tea. Suddenly, they noticed a dark thing in the water, moving steadily towards them. It came to within twenty yards, diving and resurfacing, and they distinctly saw a horrible long-necked, hump-backed creature. Miss Carberry remembers that 'the whole body had movement in it... it seemed like wormy. You know - creepy.' As Georgina Carberry and her friends hurried away from Lough Fadda, she kept looking back in case the monster had left the water and was following them. The experience caused her to have nightmares for weeks afterwards.

Lough Nahooin, near Claddaghduff, is a diminutive stretch of water, just one hundred yards long, eighty yards wide and no more than twenty feet deep, but it has become quite famous for its monster. The large, black, serpentine animal has been seen time and again. It seems quite impossible, utterly ridiculous, but then...

Like Morgawr and Nessie, the Irish creatures are, very occasionally, seen ashore. Perhaps they can worm their way overland, from lake to lake. Many of the small lakes are linked to larger ones by streams and rivers, and rivers lead eventually to the sea. In the 1890s a Connemara monster was trapped and died in a culvert between Lough Crolan and Derrylea Lough. No one would venture anywhere near the noxious carcass and it was simply left to 'melt away'. Could this be a clue towards an understanding of the nature of the peiste?

In 1980 I returned to the Kingdom of Kerry, fully intending to raise the 'great wurrum' of Lough Leane. Chris was with me, and we had arranged to meet some other members of our monster-hunting band at Puck Fair.

Killorglin's *Aonach an Phuic* is reputed to be the most ancient fair in Ireland. A great hairy male goat is captured in the mountains, then paraded through the town with great ceremony. He is hoisted to the top of a tall wooden tower, built in the square, and a young maiden crowns him as the only true 'King of all Ireland'. King Puck, the horny one, an authentic pagan deity.

On Gathering Day, five members of the Shiels tribe - Chris and myself, daughter Meig, and our two sons, Gareth and Ewan - having wandered from Cornwall, France and Germany, gathered together in Sheahan's Bar, where we met up with Meig's mandolin-picking boyfriend, Ashley, and fell in with a group of travelling people, tinkers and gypsies. Puck Fair is traditionally the occasion when travellers from all over Ireland, and far beyond, meet up, exchange family news and gossip, make some money, have a few drinks, sing a song or two, and maybe enjoy the odd bout of fisticuffs. It is, as we say, 'great crack'. At Sheahan's, we met two young witches, Eileen and Mary O'Donoghue, who were 'dukkerin', telling fortunes, and enjoying themselves in great style. They joined our gang.

Meanwhile, near Ballyferriter on the Dingle peninsula, Miss Kathleen O'Shea was terrified by a 'giant black animal like a bat' which suddenly flew up from behind a hedge. In the same area, around the same time, an ancient standing stone ceased to stand.

Back at Puck Fair, three wild nights and days were spent making music, clowning and conjuring, all over town. On the last day, we ran into Seamus Creagh, known as 'Famous Seamus', the brilliant traditional fiddle-player. He promised to meet us later, in Killarney.

A couple of nights after leaving King Puck and Killorglin, the bold dragon-hunters pitched their tents in a secret place amongst the trees by Lough Leane. We built a fire, cooked and consumed a great cauldron of stew, then passed round a jug of poteen. Just before midnight, the O'Donoghue sisters began to sing an eerie song in Shelta, the secret tongue of the tinkers. I could not understand a single word of it, a strange lonely air, ending very abruptly. Just as suddenly, a strong wind blew up, howling through the trees and lifting spray from the lough waves. I piled more logs on the fire, which roared bright as a furnace. Then I spoke my own special words, and the four women, sky-clad, walked into the water, calling up the beast [see pl. 21a].

No water monster showed itself. At least we didn't see one.

The storm grew more violent, the wind screaming through the woods like a banshee, tree branches creaking and snapping, and strange animal sounds, barking and crying. Those four brave witches ran, shivering, ashore and quickly dressed, huddling round the fire, grabbing the poteen. Then it began to rain. We buried the fire and took to our fiercely flapping tents.

The next day dawned bright and calm. Mary and Eileen sang a morning song and we broke our fast with eggs and rashers, washed down with strong tea. Only Meig volunteered to take a dip that day. Still, no peiste appeared, but, as Meig was swimming, a large black and white bird flew up from the lough and soared overhead for a minute before vanishing behind the trees. It was the size and shape of an albatross. Mary and Eileen insisted that it was *ean sidh*, a fairy bird. I don't know. It looked like a flesh and feather albatross to me, however unlikely a visitor to Killarney lakes such a bird might be.

Later that day, in Killarney, after leaving the others to their own devices and vices, Chris and I went to Courtney's Bar, where we found Seamus Creagh and his friend, Pauline Dodds. They had a strange tale to tell. Around twelve of the clock the previous night, Seamus and Pauline had been driving into Ballyvourney, just over the Kerry–Cork border between Killarney and Macroom, when a large animal stepped into the road, in the full glare of the car's headlamps. 'It was grey in colour,' said Pauline, 'with a shaggy coat and tufted ears'. As soon as they got home, Seamus and Pauline searched through an encyclopedia until they found a picture of some animal which looked like the one they had seen... a lynx.

There may be significance in the fact that Seamus Creagh and Pauline Dodds encountered their Munster lynx at the very same time that the witches and I were trying to raise a beastie in Lough Leane. While over the water in Britain, mysterious big cats were appearing hither and thither, devouring sheep and worrying farmers. Several frightening felines were seen near Loch Ness.

On the night of 18 August, Chris, Meig, Ashley Drees and I returned to our secret camp-site by Lough Leane. Around midnight, we were visited by a salmon poacher, an old man, who, quite casually, told us that he had seen the lough monster earlier that evening. 'What kind of animal is it?' I asked. 'It is no kind of animal at all,' he replied, 'it is a spirit, a pooka.' I asked him how many lakes in Ireland were haunted by such spirits. 'Every last one,' he said, 'and that's the truth, so it is.'

Now the pooka, or puca, is a shape-shifting fairy creature which can appear in many forms, as a horse, a bull, an eagle, a bat, or a goat. Its name, derived from *poc*, a he-goat, is related to the Welsh Pwca and, of course, to Puck. No doubt, should he choose to do so, the pooka could metamorphose into a convincing 'wurrum'.

Back in Cornwall, after ten days of preparatory rituals, we raised Morgawr again, on 9 November, from a work-boat in the Carrick Roads. A black hump was seen by two witnesses, apart from myself, but missed entirely by a BBC TV film crew, roaring around in a high-speed craft [see pl. 8b].

The following Thursday, I was having a couple of lunchtime pints at the Globe in Falmouth, when a man in his late fifties or early sixties came up and introduced himself as Mr Martin. He told me he had seen Morgawr at about four o'clock the previous afternoon, from Rosemullion Head. He described the creature as gigantic, 'with a body like a whale and a neck like a python'. The same day, Mr Martin's daughter and grand-daughter saw some thing very like the Owlman, flying into the trees near Grebe Beach. My daughter, Kate, chose the early morning of 13 November to try a sky-clad swim near the south wall of Pendennis Point. In the first light of dawn, she saw a dark hump rise up, about three hundred yards off-shore. It was followed by a smaller hump, then a long neck. The Morgawr was over twenty five feet long. For all I know, it could have been a pooka!

On 3 December, 19-year-old Wendy Mann of Drumnadrochit saw a big 'cat-like beast' running across the Lewiston road, close to Castle Urquhart. On the same day, a Drumnadrochit grocer, Jimmy Cameron, driving towards Inverness on the A82, saw Nessie just twenty yards from the shore. 'Its head and neck,' he said, 'were about three feet out of the water and behind was a long body. Its skin was black and appeared smooth'. More pookas?

Much of 1981 was taken up travelling around Ireland, doing our theatrical stuff in Dublin, Kildare, Offaly, Roscommon, Galway, Clare, Tipperary, Limerick, Cork and, eventually, Kerry,

Master Pwca or Max Ernst?
André Breton recognized Ernst's
bird-like profile in this coalminer's
portrait of a Welsh goblin.
[From *British Goblins*
by Wirt Sikes, 1880.]

just in time for Puck Fair. One of the first people to greet us, in Killorglin on Gathering Day, was Rich Crowe, the Chicago ghost-hunter, who was seeking the curious Kerry Carabuncle. On Scattering Day I met a young Mayo man called Pat Kelly, who was more than a wee bit interested in the monster-raising exploits of the Shiels band. There was something strange about him. He seemed to know more about us than we would really want any outsider to know. He offered to assist us at Lough Leane, but his offer was politely declined. After Puck, we returned to Killarney, and attempted once again to invoke the peiste, but we saw little more than a few unusual disturbances breaking the smooth surface of the water.

Much later we heard that, during our experiments, Lough Leane's beastie had been photographed by the mysterious Mr Kelly [see pl. 22a].

Kelly waited for more than four years before he sent me a copy of his unique photograph. By this time, he was living in the United States, and had been visiting a wizard friend of mine in Chicago when he airmailed the picture. My friend, known as Masklyn [see pl. 12d], told me that Mr Kelly made some rather startling assertions. Here are a few details from his curriculum vitae...

Patrick O'Talbot Kelly was born near Cong, between Lough Corrib and Lough Mask, Co. Mayo. He seriously claims to be a direct descendant of Edward Kelly, notorious scryer to the Elizabethan magician Dr John Dee. Patrick's father, Laurence, is supposed to have known Aleister Crowley. Kelly Senior met the 'Great Beast' in Paris in 1933, shortly after Crowley had left his Abbey of Thelema, eluding Mussolini's fascists in 'a cloak of invisibility'. Laurence Kelly said that Crowley was very interested in the Loch Ness Monster which, at that time, was hitting the headlines. Crowley recalled his Boleskine period, and claimed to have raised monstrous spirits there whilst practising the Abramelin Ritual, over thirty years earlier. Patrick Kelly visited Loch Ness with his father in 1969, and says that they both saw Nessie on 1 May, not far from Boleskine.

Kelly's story could be pure bunkum, but 'Ted' Holiday, in *The Dragon and the Disc*, reports the discovery in June 1969 of an old Turkish tapestry wrapped around a conch shell in the cemetery below Boleskine House. Holiday suspected that these curious props had been quite recently used in some form of occult ceremony. When blown, the conch produced a harsh braying note. Perhaps the Kellys, father and young son, had used that convoluted shell, emblem of Poseidon, to call up an aquatic monster on May Day 1969.

Whatever the truth behind those Loch Ness happenings, Patrick Kelly professes to have taken a picture of Lough Leane's creature in mid-August 1981, when the Shiels team was busy invoking. His photograph is remarkably similar to 'Mary F''s snaps of Morgawr, showing a dark, double-humped, long-necked shape, silhouetted against light reflected from the water's surface. There is an upright oblong shape in the bottom left corner of the picture which may or may not be the stem of a boat. Masklyn, half jokingly, has suggested it could even be my stovepipe hat! I will discuss tall hats, eventually. As for the Kelly photograph... I think it smells of soluble fish.

'Golf is of games the most mystical, the least earth bound, the one wherein the walls between us and the supernatural are rubbed thinnest.'
John Updike

EARLY in the year of 1982 I became a shamanic surrealist golfer; but in the merry month of May, my golfing career was abruptly banjaxed when I was heavily clubbed and clouted, near Falmouth's waterfront. It was all about the Malvinas/Falklands business, and my Hibernian connections. Ireland having refused to support Thatcher in her adventure, I was used as a scapegoat by a gang of patriotic English thugs. After weeks of painfully interesting treatment, my physiotherapist recommended accordion playing as being 'probably good' for a badly injured right hand. As my musical repertoire consists largely of very obviously Irish jigs, reels, polkas and hornpipes, it seemed prudent to take the advice, do what was good for me, and head back over the water to Erin.

About this time, I had a series of dreams in which my injured hand was cut off. It crawled about with an independent life of its own, like *The Beast With Five Fingers*. Someone told me that the severed hand symbolized fear of castration, and it is certainly true that I do not relish the thought of emasculation, however, the hand has other meanings too. It is a recurring theme in surrealist iconography.

It was a grand old summer, but we didn't raise a single monster. Instead, I practised raising a rope in what has to be called the Irish Rope Trick. We raised a few glasses, too. The Rope Trick, Indian or Irish, is closely related to snake-charming. They both entail the coaxing of a limp thing into becoming an upstanding thing. Some of the techniques involved can be usefully applied to monster raising. The symbolism is obvious, as is the fact that Gellerite spoon bending has the opposite effect and is to be carefully avoided.

The so-called 'Geller Effect' was anticipated by Dali in his famous painting *The Persistence of Memory* (1931). The Catalan writer Josef Pla has suggested that Dali is descended from an Irishman, Peter O'Daly, who was governor of the Medas Islands, south of Cadaques. An interesting theory, and the O'Dalys are, traditionally, poets. Another Irishman, Peter Moore, was Dali's *homme d'affaires* for several years. Then of course, Dali is an anagram of the *Dail*, Ireland's parliament. But I'm wandering...

1983 was the fiftieth anniversary of Nessie's headline-hitting debut, but I devoted most of my monster-raising energies to the Irish creatures.

Some forty-odd miles north-west of Galway town, below Beanna Beola, on the way to Clifden, is a chain of dragon-haunted waters: Lough Inagh, Derryclare Lough and Ballynahinch Lake. On a warm mid-September afternoon, as I gazed at Lough Inagh, a small dark hump broke the surface, about a hundred and fifty yards from the shore. I raised my camera and just had time to take one shot before the hump submerged and vanished [see pl. 22a]. Later that day, something guided me towards Maumeen Lough, and up came another hump. Two sightings in one afternoon was incredible, but the incredible had suddenly happened.

Later, on Achill Island, Co. Mayo, I saw another peiste. Achill is quite famous for its water monsters. For at least half a century there have been sightings of a 'huge animal' in Straheens Lough, near Achill Sound, but that particular beast avoided showing itself to me. However, one day, after a lunchtime jar of stout at Keel, Chris, Kate, her boyfriend, and I strolled onto the local golf course, between Trawmore Sound and the south shore of Keel Lough. Whatever impulse had guided us there must have been quite unconscious because we were, all four, taken absolutely by surprise when a smooth, off-white, elongated hump rose gently to the surface and moved slowly eastward through the water. I remember thinking 'this is ridiculous... impossible' as I raised the camera and snapped just one shot before the weird thing submerged [see pl. 23a]. It looked rather like the 'forehead' of an albino whale, so I gave it the nickname 'Moby Mick' .

The following day, in Foxford town, I heard tales of monsters in Lough Cullin and Lough Conn. The area between the loughs is said to be haunted by a spectral hound. I would have been delighted to discover a great 'wurrum' in this part of Mayo, if only because my father's family were Foxford people, but I had no luck. All the same, beautiful Lough Conn had an uncanny atmospheric feeling about it.

O'Connor's, in Doolin, Co. Clare, is a mecca for traditional musicians, and I had spent a lively night there, playing the accordion and enjoying more than a few strong drinks. The morning after, I sought to clear my throbbing head by taking a stroll on the windswept Cliffs of Moher. It was there that I noticed the strange vermiform patterns in slabs of local stone [see pl. 22b]. This may have triggered something in my mind because, within a few hours, I saw my first (and last) Irish sea-serpent. I was on the road to Lehinch, and decided to take a look at the golf links, said to be haunted by Donn, the Fairy King. I met up with a pair of elderly American golfers, and we stood chatting on O'Brien's Bridge, looking across to Liscannor Bay. Then it appeared, in the estuary of the Dealagh River, a black sinuous shape. 'What's that?' asked one of my American friends. 'It's a marine peiste,' I replied, very casually. 'Is that a common animal here?' he asked. 'Quite a lot of them in the West,' said I, aiming my camera at the thing [see pl. 23b].

Some weeks later, back in Cornwall, the photographs were developed and turned out to be disappointing, mainly due to the lack of a telephoto lens. Being philosophical about these things, I suspect that, if a telephoto *had* been fitted to my camera, the 'wurrums' would have failed to appear.

In September, while I was on the trail of the Irish peiste, a Scottish woman on a cycling holiday photographed the Loch Ness Monster from a spot near Achnahannet. The picture shows a creature remarkably similar to the thing I saw and snapped from Castle Urquhart in 1977 [see pl. 20a]. I cannot decide whether to regard this similarity as reassuring or suspicious.

A photograph can never *prove* the independent physical reality of whatever is photographed. It can only present a sign.

7

SIGNS AND PORTENTS

'We were busy marrying sounds to each other in order to rebuild things, endlessly proceeding to metamorphoses, calling forth strange animals.'
Louis Aragon

I happen to be scribbling these words, in Ponsanooth, during the wet and windy, sometimes sunny, early summer of 1987; trying not to fret too much about the probable re-election of Margaret Hilda Thatcher, by reflecting on the fact that, fifty summers ago, this part of Cornwall became healthily plagued with surrealists.

Roland Penrose hosted the formidable gang, and wrote:

'The green meadows, the creeks, the moors, the logan stones, the Merry Maidens, the lighthouses, Woolworth's stores, the Goonhilly Downs, the beaches and the local pubs suffered a sudden surrealist invasion.'

The group included Eileen Agar and Joseph Bard, Paul and Nusch Eluard, Man Ray and Adie, E.L.T. Mesens, Herbert Read, Lee Miller, Max Ernst and Leonora Carrington. They all descended on the Truro River house of 'Beacus' Penrose, Roland's brother, and proceeded to call forth strange animals.

One night, Eileen Agar, Lee Miller, Nusch Eluard, and Leonora Carrington danced naked near Mylor, and probably raised the 'large snakelike creature' seen there at that very time.

Eileen Agar had already discovered a 'bird-snake' on the Dorset coast, and photographed the 'prehistoric monster' rocks, of Ploumanach, Brittany. Lee Miller pointed her camera towards 'disquieting images'. Nusch Eluard had created some strange submarine photomontages. And Leonora Carrington was obsessed with Celtic totem-beasts.

A powerful quaternity of sorceresses. But the arch sorcerer of that particular party was Max Ernst [see pl. 13b].

I have already mentioned the fact that Owlman makes me think of Ernst. There be dragons, too, in the works. Ernst's paintings, collages and frottages are full of weird entities. One particular canvas – *Surrealism and Painting* (1942) [see pl. 13c] – portrays surrealism itself as a monster, a viscous writhing creation, part bird, part serpent, part human, caught in the act of picture making. It contains elements of the fabulous Loplop, *le superieur des oiseaux*, Ernst's bird-headed alter ego [see next page]. Loplop–Ernst seems to know all about Owlman and Morgawr. I look to him for signs.

I must emphasize the primary importance of surrealist thinking in the business of monster-raising. Monsters are essentially surreal. Involvement with monsters is an intrinsically surrealist experience, with a high proportion of absurd, bizarre, disordered, or irrational elements. Monsters are mysteries, loaded with latent meaning. In order to clearly *see* a monster, interior and exterior obstacles between the seer and reality must be removed, the antimonies wiped out. Max Ernst has said that men might fly if only they stopped allowing themselves to be tamed. 'Normal' perception has been tamed. Monsters can only be truly seen with a savage eye. When that eye is a photographer's, monsters are sometimes captured on film.

The camera, still or cinematographic, can be a magical instrument, a tool for visionaries and alchemists. It encourages surreal perception and invites things to happen. The lycanthropically named Fox-Talbot and the enlightened brothers Lumière advanced the art and craft of conjuring most marvellously.

On St Patrick's Day 1856, the Rev. Charles Lutwidge Dodgson [see pl. 14a] decided to purchase his first camera, because he wanted another occupation beyond 'mere reading and writing'. The very next morning, he spent just £15 with T. Ottewill of Charlotte Street, Caledonian Road, and plunged into his 'one recreation'. Dodgson's favourite photographic subject was little girls, and his favourite little girl was Alice Pleasance Liddell [see pl. 14b], daughter of the Dean of Christ Church Cathedral, Oxford. Dean Liddell eventually, in 1922, made his mark by posthumously and

Loplop – the androgynous alter ego of Max Ernst – presents squid-like, plant-like, bird-like, and even human qualities. [Drawing by Max Ernst.]

preternaturally projecting a self-portrait in the form of a white stain, onto one of the cathedral walls.

Aleister Crowley produced a book of pornographic verse, called *White Stains*. Crowley's magical master, for a time, was Samuel Liddell Mathers. Crowley was vilified in a sensational scandal-sheet called *The Looking Glass*. Dodgson, better known as Lewis Carroll, wrote *Alice Through the Looking Glass*. Ley hunters will appreciate the significance of the 'dod' name, *Dod*gson, and the 'ley' name Crow*ley*.

Then we come to Cotting*ley*, and the famous fairy photographs [see pl. 15]. In 1922 Sir Arthur Conan Doyle's book about the Cottingley pictures, *The Coming of the Fairies*, was published by Hodder. In the same year, the creator of Sherlock Holmes experimented with 'automatic writing', as did the early surrealist group, and Alice Liddell sent for a set of the Cottingley photographs. Still in 1922, Conan Doyle astounded a gathering of the Society of American Magicians, at the Hotel McAlpin, New York (he was there as a guest of Harry Houdini), when he screened a reel of test footage for the first film version of *The Lost World*, showing 'extraordinarily lifelike' prehistoric monsters. In his introductory speech, Doyle said: 'These pictures are not occult, but they are psychic because everything that emanates from the human spirit or human brain is psychic.'

That very same year, the review *Littérature* published André Breton's text, *Entrée des mediums*, describing the automatic writing and drawing sessions of the proto-surrealists. They were photographed by Man Ray, and painted by Max Ernst, whose 1922 canvas *Au Rendez-vous des Amis*, is a superb group portrait. It includes Louis Aragon, who would soon produce a perfect French translation of Carroll's *The Hunting of the Snark*. I mention these things because these things should be mentioned.

Alice, underground, drank a magic potion and shrunk to fairy-size, then nibbled the magic mushroom and grew a serpentine neck, which 'curved in a graceful zigzag'. A shamanic shape-shifter, communicating with animals, familiars, tricksters. She was and is both bewitched and bewitching. When she passed *Through the Looking Glass*, Alice was told: 'With a name like yours, you might be any shape, almost.' It is a name favoured by witches, as is its diminutive, Alison. The English surrealists have been called 'the children of Alice'. She is their muse, inspiring them as Alice Liddell inspired Dodgson. She is Breton's ideal, enchanting *femme-enfant*, the woman-child, possessing direct access to the unconscious, through the magic mirror, and *L'Écriture Automatique*.

I mentioned Guinness, the magic potion, earlier. Some years ago I noticed that its name contained the message: G-U-IN-NESS. G-U meaning 'Great Unknown', 'Grotesquely Upstanding', or some such suggestive phraselet, pointing to the monster in the porter-dark waters of Loch Ness [see pl. 20]. I asked Arthur Guinness and Sons if they fancied giving me financial backing for a properly equipped Loch Ness Monster hunting expedition; but, after long and careful consideration, they politely replied in the negative. I drowned my disappointment in Guinness, at my Ponsanooth local, the Stag Hunt, now run by a Dublin couple, Dermot and Maeve Maguire. I will not go into the eventual financial scandal of the 'Guinness Affair', but it may have been just one result of upsetting a wizard. Back in the winter of 1933/4, when Nessie was regularly in the news, Guinness produced a series of advertisements, fea turing Alice in Monsterland, accompanied by the White Knight, equipped with a lobster-pot.

> 'What is the lobster-pot for?' Alice asked in a tone of great curiosity.
> 'Well,' said the White Knight, 'it's an invention of my own. I'm going to look for this Monster, you see, and it might come in handy.'
> 'It's not very likely the Monster would turn out to be a lobster,' said Alice.
> 'Not very likely, perhaps,' said the Knight, 'but it's as well to be prepared for *everything*. That's why I'm carrying this Guinness - nothing like Guinness with Lobster, you know. And there's another reason.'
> 'What is that?' asked Alice.
> 'Well, something tells me I'm going to need a Guinness,' said the Knight. 'The Monster might put up a resistance - and who can resist a Guinness?'

In the eighteenth century, the Guinness Brewery at St James's Gate, Dublin, took its water from the *Dodder*.

In 1878, Alice Liddell visited the Scottish Highlands. She travelled from Inverness, via the railway and Strome Ferry, to Skye, where the Liddells were guests of the Macleods of Dunvegan Castle. With her two sisters, Alice spent a lot of time in the castle's famous 'Fairy Tower'. I wonder if she heard tales about the strange creatures in Loch Brittle, Loch Scavaig, Loch Dubhrachan, and other haunted waters on or around the Isle of Skye.

Guinness built a new brewhouse in Dublin that year.

While Alice was in Scotland, Dodgson began to photograph young girls in their 'favourite dress of nothing'. An unusual, not to say dangerous, venture for a shy Victorian clergyman. Coming up against some hostile reactions from mothers whose daughters he wished to photograph in the nude, Dodgson abandoned photog-raphy altogether after 1880, the year in which Alice Liddell married Reginald Hargreaves.

In 1933, the year of Nessie's debut in the mass media (as it existed then), Mrs Alice Hargreaves was given a special showing of a new film from Paramount Studios, *Alice in Wonderland*. It starred Charlotte Henry, with Gary Cooper as the White Knight, Bing Crosby as the Mock Turtle, and W.C. Fields as Humpty Dumpty. In the same year, *King Kong* was premiered, featuring spectacular stop-motion animation by Willis O'Brien, who had been responsible for those dinosaurs in Conan Doyle's *The Lost World* a decade earlier. Also in 1933, Guinness purchased the land for a new brewery at Park Royal, North West London. This was the year that Adolf Hitler came to power, and Salvador Dali began to have erotic dreams about the newly appointed chancellor of Germany. Breton and the other surrealists strongly disapproved of Dali's oneiric Nazified fantasies, and ticked him off accordingly. In 1933, Aleister Crowley arrived in Paris. Tweedledum and Dr Dee are mixed up in this, somewhere, too.

Were those 1933 sightings of the Loch Ness Monster truly portentous? Did the ominous peiste actually point to the pestilence of Nazism? Perhaps. It is ironic that the pre-Christian Celts regarded the swastika as a symbol of good fortune.

Conan Doyle's historical novel *Sir Nigel* opens with a macabre description of the medieval Black Plague. A purple cloud appears over Britain, and rain, thick as blood, falls on the diseased landscape. The early passages are reminiscent of Matthew Phipps Shiel's *The Purple Cloud*, published in 1901, five years before *Sir Nigel* appeared. Shiel, an Irishman born in the West Indies, was known as the King of Redonda, an islet near Antigua. Because of the tribal connections, I should be regarded as pretender to that particular throne. Incidentally, Shiel sometimes wrote as 'Gordon Holmes'. In his *An Exaltation of Larks, or The Venereal Game*, James Lipton quotes from *Sir Nigel* a passage concerning 'terms of venery', or collective nouns associated with the hunt. Lipton's book is illustrated with dozens of bizarre engravings, including representations of a parliamentary host of Owlman. Obviously, I take this as a sign that it contains something relevant to my own particular venereal game. Monster hunters should know the correct group term for their quarry. We already have a knot of worms or serpents, I suggest a pestilence of dragons. In the middle ages, it was believed that a plague was conveyed in the air and that it visually resembled a dark mist or fog carrying death and destruction. Plague clouds were often associated with dragons. In *The Highlands and Their Legends*, Otta Swire tells us that, as a child, she heard of an eerie 'thing' seen around Urquhart Bay, 'a great dark shapeless mass, brooding over the waters, dreaming of evil'. Remember Crowley's conjuration of 'shadowy shapes' at Boleskine. More signs.

> *'Sometimes we see a cloud that's dragonish.'*
> **Shakespeare**

IT is said that the stones for building Castle Urquhart were
carried to the site by a coven of Glen Urquhart witches. They
used to hurl imprecations at their ganger from the Rock of
Curses, near Tychat Farm. A curse, of course, is a peste. The witches
used to gather for their sabbats at another rock known as The Harp,
which reminds me of the Melusinean Lady Pengersick, strumming
for the Mounts Bay serpents. It makes me think of Guinness, too.
The harp is a female instrument, symbolizing the feminine
principle. The majority of stringed musical instruments are female,
whilst most wind instruments, including the deep-voiced serpent,
are phallic.

Tweedledum and Tweedledee were, originally, nicknames
given to the musicians Bononcini and Handel who, in 1725, were
locked in a feud. Observers found it hard to see any real difference
between the antagonists. In 1987, the names were applied to David
Owen and David Steele, the odd alliance. According to Eric
Partridge, a tweedle is a dummy diamond ring, or a confidence
trick, making a tweedler a con man. Tweedly music is high pitched
and fidgety, usually played on a fiddle. In Looking Glass Land,
Alice thought that Tweedledum was frightened of his broken rattle
because he saw it as a rattle-*snake*. When Dum and Dee were about
to have their battle, 'a monstrous crow' flew down and scared them.
It scared Alice too, though she 'wished' it into existence. 'What a
thick black cloud that is!' she said. 'And how fast it comes! Why,
I do believe it's got wings!'

Alice ran a little way into the wood, and stopped under a large
tree. 'It can never get me *here*,' she thought: 'it's far too large to
squeeze itself in among the trees...'

According, again, to Partridge (a loaded name in itself),
during World War One, an 'Alice' was a dummy tree, an observer's
disguise, difficult to detect. Its appellation stems from Bunn's song
Alice, Where Art Thou?, which was later used as the title for a
Carrollian Guinness book, beautifully illustrated by Antony
Groves-Raines, in 1952.

The Jabberwock, a bit of an old dragon if ever I saw one, 'came
whiffling through the tulgey wood' in Alice's Looking Glass poem,
and seemed to fill her head with ideas. Somebody killed something,
ritually. Trees, woods, old greenery magic. Monstrous birds and
young girls. Dodgson himself played the part of a bird-man, the
Dodo, in Wonderland.

Roy Gasson, editor of *The Illustrated Lewis Carroll*, affirms
that Dodgson 'was sexually attracted to little girls'. I think it
obvious that he loved Alice Liddell especially, and suffered from
a peculiarly Victorian version of *l'amour fou*. This relates to
serpent-dragons in Freudian terms, and Freud tends to be rightly
closer 'to the bone' than Jung and his mystical acolytes. Falling

down rabbit holes, or into a pool of tears, getting a foot stuck up a chimney, and becoming bigger or smaller, is interesting dream-stuff for a stuttering Oxford cleric who did not sleep too soundly.

A hare is a witch creature, a lunar animal, and the madness of hares in March is the result of sexual excitement. A hatter's mental aberrations could be caused by the absorption of mercury compounds which were used in the tanning of felt. 'Mad as a cut snake' used to be a popular expression too.

I harp on certain themes here only because of their essential relevance.

Imaginative artists, such as Dodgson, Conan Doyle, Joyce, Breton, Stoker, Lautréamont, Ernst, O'Brien, and many others (including myself), oneiromantically invoke Jabberwocks, Snarks, Boojums, and variations on these psychomorphogenetic themes. Creatures great and small occurring without, let us hope, God's help. A young woman called Alice Moriarty hoodwinked Conan Doyle, in New York, in 1922. Eleven years earlier, Sherlock Holmes became a shade, ghost, or spirit tec, when he took command of *The Pursuit of the House Boat* in John Kendrick Bang's story about ethereal doings on the Styx. Bang, one supposes, did not accept the undoubted fact that Holmes had physically survived well beyond *The Final Problem*. In 1911, of course, Conan Doyle was writing *The Lost World*.

In 1928 Sir Arthur Conan Doyle saw 'a young plesiosaurus' off Aegina. It was very much like the creature seen by J. Mackintosh Bell nine years earlier near the Old Man of Hoy. Hoy? That rings a bell!

Of course you see what I am doing: stressing certain relationships between events, names, sounds, visions, and so on, selectively and subjectively. My 'evidence' is prejudiced, but no more than any other monster hunter's. Alice and Holmes seem to play seminal roles in the game.

Samuel Rosenberg, in his clever Freudian analysis of the Sherlock Holmes mysteries *Naked is the Best Disguise*, links *The Red Headed League* with *Alice's Adventures Under Ground* (the original title of the Wonderland tale). Conan Doyle's would-be bank robber, Spaulding, is a burrowing fake photographer. Rosenberg writes:

> ... suddenly Spaulding reminds us of the rabbit which the immortal Alice followed down the hole into the allegorical Wonderland. Is this Doyle's subtle hint of the allegory awaiting the reader who follows Spaulding down into the cellar and through the underground tunnel into the bank? The similarity between Spaulding and Alice is heightened when we recall that Holmes and Watson, who almost always travel by cab, go to look at the thief and the scene of the crime by Underground.

Rosenberg smiles knowingly at Spaulding's pretended interest in

amateur photography, quoting the line: 'Oh... never such a fellow
for photography. Snapping away, and then diving into the cellar
like a rabbit in its hole to develop his pictures'. Having tipped a
wink in the direction of Dodgson, Rosenberg shrewdly observes
that photography is: 'a nearly perfect paradigm of sex and
reproduction: desire, penetration, fertilization, gestation, and
birth.' Conan Doyle, according to his biographer, Charles Higham,
'revelled in amateur photography'.

Photography documents convulsed, configured, and coded
reality. It does not interpret, it *presents*.

My 1977 photographs of 'a thing seen in Loch Ness' are, in
themselves, simply that. They present something which invites interpretation, something which may or may not be a creature unknown to, or unclassified by, science. I strongly suspect that the
'something' is the Loch Ness Monster, but whether or not the Loch
Ness Monster exists as an organic animal is still a complex problem.
If there is a point involved, it is heavily moot. I try to view the whole
subject with a savage, sometimes winking, eye.

Sir Arthur Conan Doyle died in 1930, three years before
Nessie became a celebrity. Had he lived, I am sure Sir Arthur would
have been fascinated by the happenings at Loch Ness. In a 1969
film, *The Private Life of Sherlock Holmes*, the Great Detective
finally encountered the Great Beastie in the form of a five-ton
animated model, which eventually sank during a gale [see pl. 19b].

It is amusing to note that the book *Houdini and Conan Doyle*
was written by two people with the surnames Ernst and Carrington.
It may also be worth mentioning the fact that Sir Thomas
Drummond Shiels, like Conan Doyle an Edinburgh physician,
photographer and politician, was the son of a lady called Nessie
Campbell. I had an Aunt Nessie, my mother's sister; and my father's
name is Thomas D. Shiels. The character of Sherlock Holmes was
based largely on Conan Doyle's mentor at Edinburgh University,
Dr Joseph Bell. In 1950 Arthur Liddell, Baron Ravensworth,
married Wendy Bell, a name which brings to mind yet another
Edinburgh University man, James M. Barrie, close friend of Conan
Doyle, and creator of Peter Pan, Wendy and Tinkerbell. This name
game is part of the Fortean pursuit of 'lexilinks', a term concocted
by A.J. Bell. Bell and Howell cameras were used to film *The Lost
World*. Bell's Scotch Whisky is now part of the Guinness empire.
This can go on and on, so I will call a halt, after a quick reminder
that it was Bellerophon who killed the Chimera.

In discussing such things as sea serpents, the Loch Ness
mystery, the Owlman, and the Little People, we find ourselves in
the realm of the 'weird', 'eerie', or 'uncanny'. They engender a
peculiar *frisson*, a feeling of uneasy excitement. Lewis Carroll, in
his preface to *Sylvie and Bruno*, wrote:

I have supposed a Human being to be capable of various psychical states, with varying degrees of consciousness as follows: (a) the ordinary state, with no consciousness of the presence of Fairies; (b) the 'eerie' state in which, while *un*conscious of actual surroundings, and apparently asleep, he (i.e. his immaterial essence) migrates to other scenes, in the actual world, or in Fairyland, and is conscious in the presence of Fairies.'

Carroll seems to equate the 'eerie' state with the surreal or mediumistic trance state, during which 'visions' and 'out-of-body' wanderings are experienced. 'Eerie' or 'uncanny' states, feelings, and atmospheres are often associated with things which would or should *normally* remain hidden, or secret, beginning to reveal themselves. Freud used the German word *unheimlich* to describe the 'eerie' or 'uncanny' areas of the psyche, hidden deep in the unconscious and often repressed, but which can be brought to light by the analyst, artist or shamanic seer. Jung and his pupils have suggested that perhaps the monsters of modern 'horror' films are distorted versions of archetypes that will no longer be repressed (I cannot resist linking Jung with *Mighty Joe Young* and remember the big ape could only be tamed by a young girl playing *Beautiful Dreamer*).

I am sure that there is a connection between the release of *King Kong* in 1933 and the repeated appearances that year of the Loch Ness Monster. George Spicer readily admitted, to Rupert Gould, that he had seen the film and thought that 'his' monster was very much like the brontosaurus in *King Kong*, which emerges from a fog-shrouded swamp. Kong, the giant ape, a truly supersasquatch, is another classic archetype. Robert Anton Wilson regards him as 'Pan Ithyphallos, right out of the collective unconscious'. The film was premiered in March, the very same month in which John and Donaldine Mackay of Drumnadrochit witnessed the 'strange spectacle' which started the whole modern Loch Ness Monster saga.

Lewis Carroll's 'Alice' books and the Cooper/Schoedsack *King Kong* are 'fairy tales', a term which is often used to describe improbable accounts of unusual happenings. Alice, shape-shifting witch-girl, plays the parts of both heroine and monster in Wonderland. 'I'm *not* a serpent!' said Alice indignantly. 'Let me alone!' But: 'all she could see, when she looked down, was an immense length of neck, which seemed to rise like a stalk out of a sea of green leaves that lay far below her.' [See next page.] Like Kong, a gargantuan Alice pushes her arm (Pat, the Irish apple-digger, calls it an 'arrum'!) through a window: 'Who ever saw one that size? Why, it fills the whole window!' Kong's great arm thrusts through the window of a New York hotel and he lifts a fainting Fay from the bed. Fay (a fairy name) Wray, as Ann Darrow, is the object of

Kong's *l'amour fou*, just as Alice, real or imagined, is the object of Dodgson/Carroll's repressed mad love. Kong carries his 'little girl' to the top of the phallic Empire State Building, and meets his doom. 'Oh, no. It wasn't the airplanes,' says Carl Denham at the end of the picture, 'It was *Beauty* killed the Beast'. Dodgson tried to kill the 'beastly' Jabberwockian side of his sexual nature, a whiffling burbling paedophiliac beast, locked in the deepest psychic dungeon, but he failed. His books are packed with surreally libidinous imagery, as is *King Kong*.

So-called 'primitive' cultures sometimes regard the photographic camera as a 'stealer of souls'. At the same time, a telephoto lens is often regarded as the phallic extension of a magically 'life-creating' thing. I am tempted to link the 'one-eyed trouser snake' with the Stirn 'Secret' or 'Detective' camera, popular in the Victorian era, and designed to be 'worn concealed under clothing'... 'with the lens protruding through a buttonhole'. The Daguerreotype process used to be called 'the mirror with a memory', and a Daguerreotype image is a looking glass image, laterally reversed. These facts constantly remind me of Dodgson.

In 1833, a hundred years before Nessie was first photographed, William Henry Fox Talbot was inspired to 'invent' the modern photo-

After eating a piece of mushroom, Alice's neck extends to such monstrous proportions that she is taken for a serpent by a Pigeon. [Drawings by Carroll/Dodgson for his *Alice in Wonderland*.]

graphic process on the shores of Lake Como.

At this point I have to recall Patrick O'Talbot Kelly, son of Laurence O'Talbot Kelly, and mention the interesting point that Larry Talbot was *The Wolf Man*... 'with its unearthly body a twitching tomb of strange desires'... in the 1940 Universal movie. The heraldic Talbot is, of course, a hound, as is the Baskerville beast. Nicolas Meyer introduced Sherlock Holmes to Sigmund Freud and Bram Stoker. Conan Doyle and Stoker were friends. Stoker and Ellen Terry were friends. Ellen Terry and Dodgson were friends. Ellen Terry married a man named Kelly. King Kong stuck his hairy hand through a bedroom window and grabbed Sandra Shaw, who married Gary Cooper, who played the White Knight in that 1933 *Alice in Wonderland* film. Alice Cooper comes to mind, and ritual decapitation illusions presented by the Amazing Randi, who constantly battles with Uri Geller and gets upset about the Cottingley fairy photographs. It is a great pity that those pictures were not taken with a Brownie camera. Randi, by the way, is a Nessie fan.

During Dodgson's lifetime, and especially during the years in which his obsessions were expressed, sea-serpents were sighted regularly in British coastal waters. Perhaps Dodgson's dreamings may have encouraged some of these happenings.

Dodgson is linked with Whitby, the Yorkshire fishing port. Bram Stoker's *Dracula*, too, has connections with the place. Whitby, and its fishing community, was much photographed by nineteenth and early twentieth century cameramen (Frank Sutcliffe being, probably, the best remembered). Sherlock Holmes met Dracula in my 1977 play *Spooks*, or rather more accurately, I should say that Holmes *became* Dracula. Certain members of the cast were very familiar with Whitby and its interestingly named headland of Kettleness. Maurice Richardson has said of *Dracula*: 'from a Freudian standpoint and from no other does the story really make sense.' Stoker is supposed to have dreamed the original concept after a late supper of dressed crab. *Dracula* has been over-psychoanalyzed, and there is little point in going over the same well dug ground. But... just take a swift look at Bram Stoker's last book: *The Lair of the White Worm*.

With what his great-nephew, Dan Farson, has called 'a remarkable prophecy of the Loch Ness Monster', Stoker wrote about 'holes of abysmal depth, where any kind and size of antediluvian monster could find a habitat'. One such monster is the 'foul White Worm', a bizarre serpent which has 'obtained control' over the body of the beautiful Lady Arabella March. The White Worm *becomes* Lady Arabella, that is to say the lady turns into a Melusine, a Lamia, like Cornwall's Lady Pengersick. Farson comments on the 'Gothic surrealism' of Stoker's weird tale, with its 'almost ludicrous' plot. True, the book is a ridiculous, badly written, formless mess, but is fascinating from a surrealist point of view.

In their entertainingly perceptive booklet, *The Meaning of the Loch Ness Monster*, Roger Grimshaw and Paul Lester point to 'the obvious affinities which exist between our monster entrepreneurs and that other archetype of western individualism and investigative enterprise - the private detective. Both utilise deductive procedures to uncover facts whose significance has been overlooked by authority, scientific or legal'. They go on to discuss the monster in Freudian psychoanalytic terms, finding correspondences 'between monster attributes and symbols of unconscious desire - the body and the phallus'.

Ronald Binns, in *The Loch Ness Mystery Solved*, recognizes the 'strong correlation between sightings and mirror-calm conditions at Loch Ness. When the loch is a *mirror* it reflects, perhaps, images from the unconscious'.

It may be thought that such 'images from the unconscious' are impossible to photograph. Man Ray, Paul Nougé, Jacques-André Boiffard, Raoul Ubac, Marcel Marien, and fellow surrealist photographers, have proved otherwise. Freud has shown that many of the things which are used as genital symbols in mythology and folklore play the same part in dreams. He cites the airship as a 'modern' example of this. In 1982 a Goodyear airship flew over Loch Ness, and, because of its shape and size, effectively replaced the monster [see pl. 18b]. 1982's Nessie-spotting season was unusually lean.

I have to stress the difference between the involuntary projection of those 'symbols of unconscious desire', and the deliberately invocatory habits of surrealist seers. A surrealist encourages his other hallucinatory faculties, dissolving barriers between the conscious and unconscious, to achieve a 'fusion of the imaginary and the real'.

Nessie certainly seems to symbolize 'the beast with two backs', in an eerie, uncanny, variety of forms, and by so doing becomes a psychic and corporeal expression of the totemic androgyne. The beast can sometimes be photographed or filmed, but only, it seems, if the camera is used, consciously, unconsciously, or surrealistically, as an invocatory device, a tool with which to capture the image of an 'object of desire'.

Surrealists, in lucidly and purposefully removing the distinctions between imagination and reality, deliberately trigger the Freudian 'uncanny', and 'regress' (as Freud would say) into an 'animistic conception of the universe', with its 'confusion' between the animate and inanimate. Professor David Bohm, the quantum physicist, informs us that 'life is implicit in what we call inanimate matter', and that 'distinctions between the animate and inanimate are only abstractions, useful in some contexts but ultimately inaccurate'. So...???

8

THE PICTISH BEAST

> *'He thought he saw an Elephant,*
> *That practised on a fife:*
> *He looked again, and found it was*
> *A letter from his wife.'*
> **Lewis Carroll**

IN its issue of 2 August 1979, the *New Scientist* published a photograph [see below] by Admiral R. Kadirgama showing an elephant swimming off the coast of Sri Lanka. This illustrated a piece in which Doctors Donald Johnson and Dennis Power jokingly suggested that sightings of 'long-necked' sea serpents and lake monsters could be misidentifications of swimming elephants. A little later, in the pages of *Fortean Times* (No.30, p67), Mike Crowley compared the Admiral's elephant with a mysterious animal-image, found on ancient stones carved by Pictish artists and known as the 'Beast', or 'Swimming Elephant'. *Living Wonders* was published in 1982 and, on page 105, authors John Michell and Robert J.M. Rickard proposed a possible link between swimming elephants, the Pictish 'Beast', and the Loch Ness Monster. In 1983 I considered the matter carefully.

Admiral Kadirgama's swimming elephant.

The Loch Ness Monster has often been described in elephantine terms... leaving aside, for the time being, the 'pink elephant' aspects of the enigma. Mr and Mrs George Spicer saw 'an abomination' with a long undulating appendage like 'an elephant's trunk', crossing the road between Dores and Foyers in the summer of 1933. When Miss Margaret Munro encountered Nessie in 1934, she said: 'the skin was like an elephant's'. In 1960, 'Torquil MacLeod' watched the monster through binoculars and likened its 'head and neck' to 'an elephant's trunk which kept moving from side to side and up and down'.

Morgawr, too, has been described in similar terms. 'Mary F' said the sea serpent 'looked like an elephant waving its trunk'. Her photographs certainly show something looking very much like Admiral Kadirgama's paddling pachyderm. The same could be said of Pat Kelly's depiction of the Lough Leane creature.

The Pictish 'Beast' or 'Elephant' [see pp114-15], at first glance, seems to be a piece of artistic invention, not at all like a real swimming elephant in spite of its archaeological name. Pictish 'symbol' stones are now grouped into two classes. Class I stones, dating from around the sixth century, are usually unshaped slabs with one or two flat faces on which the symbols are incised in line. The later Class II stones are, technically, more advanced and elaborate, often carved in low relief. The 'Elephant' appears regularly on both classes of stone, often in the company of naturalistically rendered 'normal' animals, such as bulls, horses, salmon, deer, snakes, geese, boars, eagles, and wolves. Other symbols used in conjunction with the elephant-beast include combs and mirrors, a crescent, and enigmatic shapes known as the Z-rod and V-rod.

The elephant-beast has baffled generations of scholars. It is a puzzling creature, with a 'beaked' head like a dolphin's, legs which curl spirally like the tentacles of an octopus, and a trunk sprouting from the 'forehead' and curving over its long arched back. In 1983, after studying many photographs of these curious carvings, I eventually decided that if the elephant-beast represented a *real* aquatic animal, the sinuous trunk and back of the original 'life model' would be the parts likely to have been observed most often, above the waterline, by Pictish sculptors. In which case, the creature began to appear very much like a swimming elephant. Perhaps the Picts had never actually seen the underwater section of the animal, and based their representation on intelligent speculation. Maybe the thing behaved rather like a dolphin, so they gave it a dolphin-like head. But there is nothing dolphin-like about the sharp angle at which the head was held, in line with those weirdly curling 'legs'.

I returned to the bizarre notion of a genuinely aquatic

elephant. Was it possible? Dead elephants have, from time to time, been thrown up by the ocean. One of them even arrived in Cornwall, at Widemouth Bay near Bude. In 1982 the crew of a fishing boat encountered an expired elephant floating in the North Sea off the coast of Aberdeenshire. Charles Fort was interested in beached sea monsters with elephantine trunks, and noted several examples. In *Living Wonders*, Michell and Rickard describe and illustrate a strange elephant-like carcass washed ashore at Margate, Natal, in 1922 [see below].

Then I read *The Aquatic Ape* by Elaine Morgan and became quite fascinated by the ideas she expressed. In Appendix 3, she lists eleven very good reasons why she considered the modern terrestrial elephant to be a perfect example of an ex-aquatic animal. Her reasoning seemed so logical that I instantly grabbed at the possibility of a surviving branch of the family. Very soon it became obvious that, although a relict species of marine elephant could explain many sea serpent sightings, it would not do for Nessie. Elephants, like their cousins the dugongs and manatees, are strictly herbivorous. They consume vast amounts of vegetation, and simply could not survive in the inky, plantless waters of Loch Ness.

I continued to worry about the Pictish 'Beast' with its weird beaked head and spiralling 'legs' until, one day, I saw a marvellous underwater colour photograph of a common squid, *Loligo*, cruising along, its two long tentacles withdrawn, and the eight short arms held, grouped tightly, looking for all the world like a beak! In fact, the squid's round-eyed head presented an image remarkably similar to the head of the Pictish elephant-beast. Could our mystery

The proboscidean prodigy beached at Margate, Natal, in 1922. [Drawing by Penny Miller, from *Myths and Legends of Southern Africa*, 1979.]

Left: The 'Pictish Beast' on the Rodney Stone, in the drive of Brodie Castle. **Above:** The 'Beast', accompanied by horsemen and a tail-biting serpent, appears to be tying itself in Celtic knots. Note also the V-rod and crescent on this stone in Meigle Museum, Tayside.
[Both photographs: Hamish Brown/ Janet & Colin Bord.]

animal be a mollusc, a cephalopod, a weird kind of squid or cuttlefish? There seemed to be a distinct possibility that it could.

Years ago, 'Ted' Holiday expounded his theory of a monster invertebrate in *The Great Orm of Loch Ness*; basing much of his speculation on the 'Tully Monster', or *Tullimonstrum gregarium*, a small fossil creature about 250 million years old. Dr E.S. Richardson, Curator of fossil invertebrates at the Field Museum of Natural History, Chicago, described the Tully Monster as 'a most curious prodigy' with a 'dirigible-like body', a 'long thin proboscis' and a 'spade-shaped' tail. The creature was so strange that expert palaeontologists failed to classify it in any known group, though Holiday saw it as a worm. I have never seen a worm with a tail like *Tullimonstrum*'s, but squids have tails like that (a fossil creature which could turn out to be an ancestor of *Tullimonstrum* has been found in the Burgess Shale deposit, British Columbia. It is known as *Opabinia*).

The Tully Monster has what appears to be a series of ridges along its back, rather like the ridges on the chambered shells of ammonites. According to Borradaile and Potts (*The Invertebrata*, p. 649): 'The fact is that in the most primitive cephalopod now existing there is a kind of segmentation of the body cavity and mantle organs has been taken to support the origin of the cephalopods from a metamerically segmented ancestor'. *Tullimonstrum* also has a pair of rounded lateral organs which could be eyes (Dr Richardson thought he detected retinas), but which Holiday thought were parapodia. The eyes of some cephalopods (the squid, *Bathothauma lyromma*, for example) are mounted on stalks.

Tullimonstrum may be related to Nessie but, if it is, then it is more likely to be a mollusc than a worm.

Annelid worms simply cannot reach the proportions of a Loch Ness Monster. They may, in theory, attain an impressive length, but they are banjaxed when it comes to diameter. Nessie is a bulky, hump-backed beast and, as Professor R.J. Pumphrey, of Liverpool University, wrote to Holiday: 'I can think of no physical mechanism which would lift a hump of this size out of the water *except filling it with gas*' (my italics)... collapse of stout annelid! Cephalopods have gas-operated buoyancy mechanisms.

The cephalopods come in many different shapes and sizes, from the diminutive cuttlefish, *Idiosepius*, just 15mm long, to the giant squid, *Architeuthis*, which can reach a length of well over 100 feet. They are the most highly developed molluscs, with sophisticated sensory and nervous systems, and are equipped with a directional jet propulsion tube called a hyponome. According to Professor J.E. Morton, some early cephalopods may have had a trunk-like 'suctorial proboscis, breaking down food externally as do many modern decapods by salivary enzymes' (*Molluscs*, p219).

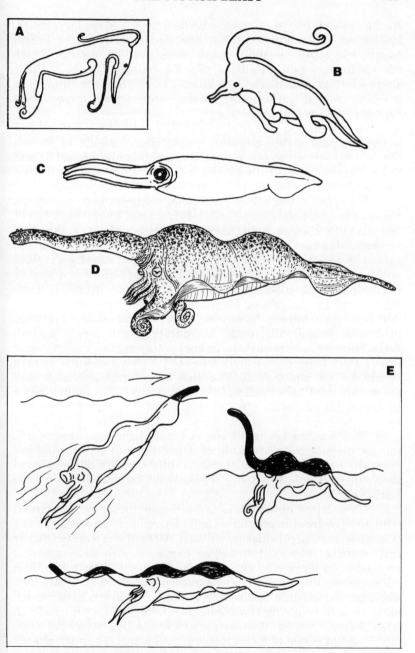

A: The 'Pictish Beast'. **B:** The 'Beast' with squid-like features emphasised. **C:** Common squid (*Loligo*). **D:** Hypothetical 'elephant squid'. **E:** The 'elephant squid' displaying Nessie-like characteristics.

Architeuthis is one of these modern decapods, and the larval form, known as *Rhynchoteuthis*, has the two long tentacles joined together as a flexible spout or proboscis, used for 'pipetting' (see *Marine Biology* by H. Friedrick, p79). Cephalopods can be brilliant shape-shifters and masters of camouflage. They are intelligent predators and, in the Mesozoic oceans, competed with large marine reptiles, such as the plesiosaurs.

So, during the winter of 1983/4, I began to form a picture of a hypothetical water monster, combining elements of Pictish 'Beast', aquatic elephant, *Tullimonstrum*, and giant squid. It had to be a cephalopod. I called it the 'elephant squid' and considered its possibilities.

My speculative beastie is a huge hump-backed coleoid. Its humps are quite elastic and inflatable, shaped by the workings of the animal's buoyancy mechanism, a flexible chain of gas-filled cavities; the cartilaginous remnants of internal shell chambers joined by a siphuncle, a tube which controls the ratio of gas to fluid within the flotation cavities. Its tail is muscular with a pair of horizontal lobes, creating a spade or leaf shape, useful as a sta-bilizer and for swimming. Replacing the two long tentacles, our decapod (or, rather, 'nonapod') has a prehensile, eversible proboscis, armed with 'teeth', and equipped with a pair of small retractile cerata or 'horns', which are sensory organs. The proboscis draws food towards the parrot-beaked mouth, where it is held firmly by six short arms. The two outer arms are large and muscular, used for crawling (like an octopus). The animal has a powerful jet propulsion funnel which can be pointed in various directions.

That was my original basic concept of the 'elephant squid', purely speculative, something of a *cadavre exquis*, bending but certainly not breaking any of the established rules of cephalopod morphology. Could it possibly, I wondered, be a candidate for the Loch Ness Monster?

My primary objection to my own hypothesis was concerned with the freshwater problem. Cephalopods are, according to the scientists, exclusively marine animals. All molluscs were originally salt water creatures, but nature came up with some amazing methods of adaption to estuarine, freshwater and terrestrial life. All members of a phylum have a basically common structure and, although the phylum Mollusca is noted for its marvellous morph-ological variety, a very few elements are involved. To quote Dr G. Alan Solem, Curator of Invertebrates at the Department of Zool-ogy, Field Museum of Natural History, Chicago: 'They are altered and combined in the various ways that form the confusingly different patterns of the major molluscan groups'. In order to adapt to a freshwater habitat, the 'elephant squid' would have to regulate

'Elephant Squid'
probable form of
cephalopod
Loch 'Ness Monster'
Shiels 1984

its body fluids accordingly. Fresh water flowing into its body
through gills or skin would tend to dilute these fluids and upset the
salt balance unless the creature had a method of secreting large
quantities of salt-free water. It may even be able to pass freely from
salt to freshwater and vice versa, anadromous or catadromous, like
a salmon or eel, by adjustment of the gill mechanisms: the chloride
cells working as devices for secreting or absorbing salt. These
changes could occur as part of a seasonal reproductive process.

The blood pigment of cephalopods is haemocyanin, a blue,
copper-containing respiratory protein that functions rather like
haemoglobin. Very little is known about the primary structure of
these copper proteins, but that's by the by. In cephalopods, the
haemocyanin is several times more concentrated than in other
molluscs, and an animal such as our 'elephant squid' would need
a highly concentrated form in order to increase the oxygen capacity
of its dark blue blood. Circulation would be boosted, as in other
cephalopods, by auxiliary hearts and contractile veins; and the
kidneys would develop, in this active predator, increasing their
nitrogen-ejection efficiency.

On rare occasions, the 'elephant squid', in its role as Nessie,
is allowed to come ashore and crawl around a bit. This means that
it must have a lung surface, in addition to gills, for aerial respira-
tion. Blood may be employed to hydrostatically extend the
proboscis, which could perhaps be used as a prepulmonary organ.
The animal's terrestrial excursions are probably limited in distance
and duration, and I assume that, if the thing exists, its 'gas balloon'
buoyancy mechanism is vital to this kind of activity. Certain species
of octopus are quite famous for their terrestrial explorations. The
'elephant squid' may share these habits. J.Z. Young has said of
Vampyroteuthis that 'it shows in the nervous system, and in the rest
of the body, a strange mixture of characters of decapods and
octopods'. The 'elephant squid' is also 'a strange mixture'. Frank
Lane, in his popular teuthological classic, *Kingdom of the Octopus*,
tells us that octopuses, on land, have been reported to move as fast
as a rapidly walking man. Then there was Pliny's famous polyp,
with arms thirty feet long, which crawled out of the sea to steal salt
fish from the beach at Cartereia, Spain. Dr Bernard Heuvelmans
correctly observes that Pliny's description of the monster suggests
a squid rather than an octopus.

Hugh Gray's historic photograph of Nessie [see pl. 16a] could
depict a mollusc of 'considerable dimensions'. I have inspected an
excellent print, from all angles, under a magnifying glass, and have
found it to have uncanny properties. Those spherical objects at the
waterline are not so convincingly round when the picture is viewed
from the sides or upside-down, not simply because of the shifting
chiaroscuro. Also, the line of the beastie's back virtually vanishes

A giant octopus doing some shipwrecking. [FPL]

when the picture is turned over. It certainly tests one's perceptual predilections with its built-in metamorphic qualities. Some people have seen the central shape as the head of a swimming dog with a stick in its mouth. As Dalí once said: 'To look is to invent'.

In 1984, when I put most of the foregoing speculations and observations together, I was attempting to 'invent' a creature which would relate to the *widest* range of Loch Ness Monster evidence, which would override the limiting objections raised concerning previous zoological candidates: giant worms, plesiosaurs, amphibians, eels, pinnipeds, roe-deer, otters, and so on. Nessie has been reported by hundreds of witnesses over the years, with such variations in size, shape, colour, skin texture, and behaviour, that only something like the 'elephant squid' could provide a possible 'flesh and blood' answer to such a confusing and seemingly self-contradictory enigma.

Between 1848 and 1974, 854 new species of cephalopod were described. That is an average of 6.7 per year. Dr Gilbert L. Voss, probably the world's leading authority on cephalopod taxonomy, has said: 'one is forced to the belief that we have nowhere near exhausted the number of undescribed species either on our museum shelves or in the sea'. Cephalopods are *weird*. Keenan Smart, who produced a BBC TV 'Wildlife on Two' programme about the things, called them *Aliens from Inner Space*. Jacques Yves Cousteau has suggested that they may have telepathic powers. J.Z. Young admits that comparatively little is known about them. G.C. Robson became mentally ill whilst attempting to classify them. I think they are marvellous.

George Spicer's impression of the Loch Ness Monster on land may be a pretty accurate picture of the thing. As well as reminding him of an elephant, he said the creature 'looked like a huge snail with a long neck'. Spicer is not the only witness to have seen Nessie as an abominable molluscan monster. Mrs Greta Finlay and her twelve-year-old son Harry saw a creature which they thought was 'horrible'. Mrs Finlay said that what astonished her, 'apart from the hideous appearance of the head, was that there were two six-inch-long projections from it, each with a blob on the end. The skin looked black and shiny and it reminded me of a snail more than anything'. Two later witnesses, Mr and Mrs Jenkyns, watched the Loch Ness Monster for about half an hour and thought it 'obscene'. 'The feeling of obscenity still persists,' said Mr Jenkyns, 'and the whole thing put me in mind of a gigantic stomach with a length of writhing gut attached.' It puts me in mind of a gigantic cephalopod with a length of writhing proboscis attached, but then I'm prejudiced.

Professor J.E. Morton has written: 'The coleoids have become adapted to swim, leap, walk, bury themselves, migrate up and down, even to fly. Ommastrephid squids in fact perform the only rocket or jet propelled flight other than man'. The Chilean giant squid can achieve an airborne velocity of 14 knots. Abbé Pernetty encountered this flying wonder when he accompanied Bougainville to the Malvinas/Falklands in 1763 and 1764. He described it as 'the biggest fish in the sea. It seizes its prey with movable barbels which it has on the ends of its nose'. Its what? He should have said 'its proboscis'. Pernetty called his 'fish' a 'cornet', and the name *encornet* is used in French for airship-shaped decapods. A plague of voracious ommastrephids hit the Pacific coast, between Monterey and San Diego, during the summers of 1934 to 1937. Several fishermen were attacked by the monsters, which were dubbed *jumbo squids*.

In October 1673, during a great storm, a huge cephalopod was driven ashore at Dingle, Co. Kerry, Ireland [see pl. 24]. Nineteen feet in length, its broad body was fringed with an undulating fin, similar to that of a cuttlefish. 'It swoom by the lappits of the mantle', according to showman James Steward, who exhibited parts of the creature. He also claimed that it had two heads, one large and one small: 'the little head it could dart forth a yard from the great, and draw it in again at pleasure'... rather like the proboscis of my speculative coleoid. The Irish zoologist A.G. More, recognizing the 'little head' as something else entirely, was apparently impressed by this aspect of the Kerry Kraken because he named it *Dinoteuthis proboscideus*... a fearsome first cousin of the 'elephant squid'.

When the preceding paragraph appeared at the end of an article on the 'elephant squid' published in *Fortean Times* (No.42), quite a lot of people assumed that I was suggesting the name *Dinoteuthis proboscideus* for my cephalopodic Nessie. I was not.

If a scientific-sounding label is needed, may I suggest *Elephanteuthis nnidnidi*?

A Celtic Nnidnid–Squid with its savage surreal eye. [Max Ernst.]

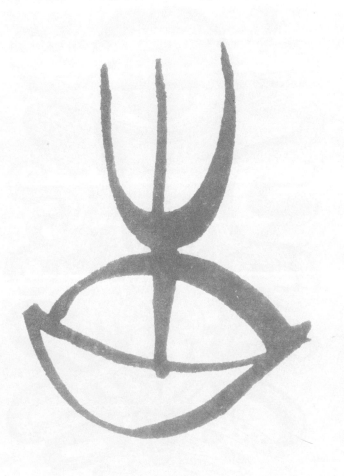

REVELATIONS

In 1985, bored with 'monsters', I deliberately experimented with psychic automatism and produced the word *NNIDNID*. Imaginatively speaking, all words are equally valuable, even *Nnidnid*, which seems to me as enigmatic and admirable as 'Dada', 'Loplop', 'jigjig', 'weewee', 'dumdum', 'metonymy', or 'crypto-zoophilia'. Every word is a mutilated marvel, and science will carry on pretending to take care of itself.

The *'poulpe au regard de soie'* is a cephalopodic surrealist totem-beast. Max Ernst, in 1929, displayed its writhing tentacular splendidness in a volcanic, multiconic, Cappadocian dreamscape **[see p129]**. The Galatian Celts, during their drunemetonic doings, wore conical hats, which must have been, sometimes, doffed in deference to the superbly eroded 'fairy cones' of Urgup, where a 'Church of Serpents' still exists.

The Picts may have had some connection with Turkey, as they, like the Turks, have affinities with the Finns. Anyone familiar with the Ural-Altaic group of languages may discover Pictish secrets. Isidore (good name) of Seville, writing in or around 600 AD, informs us that the *Picti* are so called because their bodies are tattooed with various decorative designs. It is quite probable that the same motifs which were carved on the stones were pricked on their skins. The writhing beasties on the surface plates of the Monymusk reliquary - the Brechennoch of Columba - are outlined in dots, like needle pricks. Those interlaced zoomorphs are related to the Pictish elephant-beast. Bede says that the Picts originally came from Scythia, and landed first in northern Ireland, where they married some of the local girls, then settled in the northern parts of Britain. When the Picts are discussed, it is usually the 'northern Picts' - those converted to Christianity by Columba - who receive most attention, but there were Picts in Galloway too - converted by Ninian - and they were called the *Niduari*.

Scholars fret about those puzzling Pictish symbols. The comb and mirror are mermaidenly things, so there is no great mystery as far as they are concerned. It is mainly the crescent, V-rod and Z-rod which seem to trouble people **[see pp114-15]**. The crescent, with its horns turned towards the earth, could represent the waning

moon. It is usually combined with the V-rod, which I 'read' as a
jointed ceremonial divining wand. V and Z, zigzag symbolism,
lightning and serpents. They remind me of Voodoo *vevers*: magical
designs drawn to invoke the 'loa' deity. The crescent and V-rod
combination represents a fusion of opposites, androgynous totality.
It is quite possible that Broichan, wizard to King Brude, raised a
Loch Ness Monster and 'buried' the pestilential thing, deep down
beneath the old castle. At some time, I suspect an incised stone,
bearing the image of the beast, with a crescent and V-rod, existed
on the site of Castle Urquhart.

The word 'Pict' is very similar to those fairy names: Pech, Peht
and Pixy. The Picts have also been linked with Gypsies; and a
Romany Sapengro has power over serpents. The Picts were skilled
metalworkers and excellent horsemen, as are the Gypsies and
tinkers (Tchinganes, Atsinkans, Zingari, Szgany, etc.).

I suppose silversmithery could be linked with photography.
It was an eighth century Arabian alchemist, Jabir Ibn Hayyam, who
discovered that sunlight causes certain silver compounds to
darken. Incidentally, he died in 777. William Henry Fox-Talbot
died in 1877, aged 77. I photographed Nessie in 1977. There may
be a message hidden here. Silver is connected with the moon. A
sixteenth century alchemist, Georgius Fabricus, conducted proto
photographic experiments with luna cornea, horn silver, a natu
rally occurring chloride of silver found in the mines of Freiberg,
Germany. This makes me think again of the Pictish crescent, with
its downward pointing horns. Does it signal something under
ground? A chthonic peiste, for instance?

I mentioned horses. In its lunar aspect, the horse is often
linked with lakes and the sea, associated with Poseidon, the Wild
Hunt, Herne, Epona. It is the emblem of St George, the
Cappadocian dragon-slayer. A horseshoe is a horned crescent, a
symbol of good luck. Horses play a part in this game. The water-
horse, Kelpie, and Pooka often take equine form. Connemara is
even more famous for its ponies than its peiste. Padstow comes to
mind again. The Shiels family has, for a long time, been closely
involved with horses and ponies. There has to be a strong connection between the horse and the serpent-dragon. Think again of
the interestingly named centaur, Nessus, who caused the death of
Herakles, the Hydra slayer. Then think of the Hydra.

Multi-headed serpent-dragons are quite common in ancient
myth and legend. Hydra was just one of many. There is the monster
made to burst by Daniel; the red dragon with seven heads, 'that old
serpent', seen in a vision of St John the Divine; Homer's 'dread
yelping Scylla'; the great beast killed by Perseus; the Indian
Antana, and lake-dwelling Nagas; Loton the 'close-coiling'
Canaanite; and scores of others, Hydra and its relatives were, I

The surreal, cephalopodic totem-beast reeling and writhing in Asia Minor.
[Max Ernst, *La Femme 100 Têtes*, 1929]

suspect, cephalopodic. Dr Heuvelmans, though an enthusiastic supporter of the giant-squid-as-Kraken, tends to dismiss the theory of cephalopods-as-serpent-dragons. Henry Lee, Curator of the Brighton Aquarium, authored an intelligent and imaginative little book entitled *Sea Monsters Unmasked* (1883), in which he suggested that most (not *all*) sea-serpents were actually giant squids. Lee has been maligned by many monster 'entrepreneurs', including Heuvelmans and Gould, but I think he may have come very close to the truth of the matter. *Elephanteuthis nnidnidi* could be the Great Sea Serpent after all.

In 1985 I made the momentous decision to try and produce a surrealist magazine, bearing the title *Nnidnid*. Mysterious big cats were seen prowling around the Stithians and Ponsanooth area. The *Nnidnid* plan progressed into the summer. Then Morgawr attention-seekingly rose up, again and again, in and around Falmouth Bay.

Writer Sheila Bird and her brother Dr Eric Bird, and two other witnesses, spotted the serpent-dragon on the evening of 10 July. Sheila Bird described Morgawr to the *Falmouth Packet*: '... an unfamiliar, large marine creature with a long neck, small head and large hump protruding high out of the water, with a long, muscular tail visible just below the surface, propelling itself in a north-northeasterly direction just offshore'.

The animal was estimated to be seventeen to twenty feet in length. Eric Bird said: 'Its head projected about a metre from the water, and there was a curved back about two to three metres behind. As it moved, it caused a slight ripple of the otherwise calm sea'.

A fortnight after the Birds' sighting, two campers, Jenny Halstead and Alice Lee from Hebden Bridge, Yorkshire, saw Morgawr from Rosemullion Head. Between 6:30 and 7:00 pm, they watched the weird beastie for about ten seconds before it disappeared beneath the waves. The creature was described as looking rather like 'a massive overgrown black slug'... a description of decidedly molluscan character.

The Comte de Lautréamont's intoxicating epic prose-poem *Les Chants de Maldoror* was likened by early surrealists to the 'song of an octopus riding the waves'. Its hero, Maldoror, has 'a special faculty for taking on shapes unrecognizable by expert eyes'. This shape-shifting master of disguise can, at will, become any kind of monster, human or animal. Maldoror would, I am sure, cope marvellously with the roles of Morgawr *and* Owlman. Maldoror inspires the thought that, if Morgawr is *not* an organic entity, then it is quite possible that Owlman and Morgawr are, essentially, manifestations of the same 'thing' in differing hallucinatory metamorphoses. In other words, the 'thing', in various guises, is like a psychic holographic projection in which 'interference patterns' from the unconscious interact with that electromagnetic radiation within the visible spectrum which we commonly call 'light'.

My instincts tell me that aquatic serpent-dragons, such as Morgawr and Nessie, actually exist as gigantic coleoid cephalopods *and* as misidentifications or misinterpretations of an infinite number of other things (otters, fish, deer, dolphins, seals, vegetable mats, floating logs, seaweed, boat-wakes, optical illusions, etc., etc.); *and*, further, as uncanny psychic 'visions' with an eerie 'life' of their own. Something like the Owlman, however, is almost certainly *not* a flesh-and-blood creature.

When my article on the 'elephant squid' was first published in the *Fortean Times*, Bob Rickard captioned a sketch of the hypothetical cephalopod as 'Like something out of a Lovecraftian nightmare'. Actually, the creature depicted and described is morphologically quite orthodox compared with many of the cephalopods recognized by teuthologists. Consider the strange gelatinous *Vitreledonella*; the bizarre bell-shaped *Cirrothauma*; the circular flat *Opisthoteuthis*; and the celebrated 'paper nautilus' *Argonauta*, with its most unusual sex life. All of these animals, and oodles of other scientifically examined cephalopods, appear much more weird than the 'elephant squid' or, indeed, anything dreamed up by Howard Phillips Lovecraft. Nature will always come up with a greater variety of morphological permutations than those displayed by the monsters in horror literature. Nevertheless, Lovecraft was bound to enter our story at some point.

An extremely unattractive man, H.P. Lovecraft was a racist snobbish Philistine hack with literary pretensions way beyond his very limited talent and imagination. All the same, a few of his shorter stories have a kind of demented power. He had an obsessive hatred for seafood and a fear of the sea, which may have encouraged him to endow some of his hybrid inventions, such as old Cthulhu, with cephalopodic characteristics: tentacles, for example. As I remember, I invoked his name in a piece written for the *Fortean Times* (No.27) published in 1978. It included the description of a dream in which I had seen Owlman looking very much like a scraperboard drawing of a whippoorwill, by Lee Brown Coye, illustrating Lovecraft's story *The Dunwich Horror*.

During the summer of 1978, whirring sounds, like the discordant sewing-machine calls of a group of nightjars, were heard in the woods around Mawnan Old Church. Owlman was seen that year. Lovecraft's *Caprimulgiformes* 'a-screechin' daown thar in the dark o'noonday' heralded the coming of monstrous Yog-Sothoth on Sentinel Hill. Mawnan's fern-owls, goat-suckers, or whatever they were seemed to pipe up when Owlman and/or Morgawr were about to make an appearance. This seems to me like an example of surreal 'magic circumstance'. Lovecraft, I am sure, would have detested surrealism as much as he detested (amongst many things) beer, the Irish, sensuality, and cephalopods.

André Breton enthused about a giant cephalopod featured in a 1917 Hollywood serial, *The Mystery Ship*, starring Neva Gerber and Ben Wilson. Also, like most of the surrealist group, he greatly admired the films of Louis Feuillade, especially *Fantômas*.

Those beastie boys, the entrepreneurial 'detectives', seem to be hunting a quarry as uncannily elusive as the mysterious arch-criminal Fantômas. I say this because there seem to be as many convolutions in my personal experiences on the monster trail as in any Fantômas scenario. Like the Loch Ness Monster, like Maldoror, Fantomas always eludes capture and final identification. He is a surrealist hero because he breaks the rules, constantly outwitting the forces of 'law and order', spreading terror amongst the bourgeoisie. The Loch Ness Monster, and other 'outlandish' creatures, also break the rules, bamboozle the 'experts', operate outside the accepted laws of nature and science, and have been known to terrorize whole communities.

I repeatedly refer to detective stories, 'nonsense' tales, horror films, and the like, because they contain so many clues relating to the monster mystery. Popular works of 'imaginative fiction' can tell us a great deal about ourselves: our private anxieties, repressed desires, and secret horrors. My ten-year pursuit of the serpent-dragon has demonstrated, time and again, that nothing is quite what it initially seems to be. Surrealism has given me a 'savage eye' with which to try and stare the monsters out. Like Fort, the surrealists are constantly fascinated by the odd relationships between things, rather than the things themselves. Baudelaire wrote of the imagination perceiving 'the intimate and secret connections between things, correspondences and analogies'.

In 1985, remember, Morgawr was seen by two Bird people, and a young woman called Alice.

James Joyce, in *Finnegans Wake* (the lexilinkers' bible), writes of Alice as 'the shielsome bridelittle', 'Selicas through their laughing classes becoming poolermates in laker life'. Alice, as 'addle liddle phifie', becomes A.L.P. (Anna Livia Plurabelle)... 'Alis, alas, she broke the glass!' Joyce links Padstow's Obbyoss and the great 'wurrum' when he writes 'Ess Ess. O ess, Warum night!', and 'Lang Wang Wurm'. 'The goat king of Killorglin' is there, too, in Earwicker's dream, along with some 'Spish from the Doc'. Joyce roots out 'Brimstoker' for 'Dracula's nightout', and Holmes... 'Sherlook is lorking for him'. King Arthur becomes Arthur Guinness, and the Cork-brewed stout, Beamish, is linked with the luciferous Jabberwock decapitator. 'Enfantomastic' Fantômas rubs black-clad shoulders with 'Lewd's carol', while oneiric 'mythyphallic' monsters abound. The *Wake* is a rich source of semiotic pointers and connections for the wide-awake hunter of Snarks *or* Boojums.

Sylvia Beach first published Joyce's masterwork. 'Lewis Carroll' may have predicted this in his title *Sylvie and Bruno*. Giordano Bruno, the 16th century Italian philosopher, burnt at the stake as a heretic, is very important to the *Wake*). Sylvia's sister, Cyprian, was a movie actress and portrayed Belle-Mirette in Feuillade's *Judex*, a serial made as a weird response to moral criticism of *Fantômas* and *Les Vampires. Judex* may have inspired the Shadow, a black-cloaked figure mentioned in the first pages of John Keel's book on Mothman, *The Mothman Prophecies*. Clues beget further clues and 'secret connections between things'. The word 'cyprian' is linked with the orgiastic worship of Aphrodite on Cyprus. Aphrodite, 'born of the sea', rides a mollusc shell.

Peter Tremayne (pseudonym of a distinguished Celtic scholar) has written some Dracula stories, and two romping horror novels about serpent-dragons: *The Curse of Loch Ness* and *The Morgow Rises*. Morgow/Morgawr, like Stoker's White Worm, is an 'underground' (and 'underwater') creature, inhabiting old mine workings. Just a few miles from where I live, in Cornwall, there is a tin-mining area called White Alice. Young Cornish people used to perform a curious dance, at the Midsummer 'feasts', known as the Serpent's Coil; obviously a type of labyrinthine ritual. A turf maze is sometimes called a 'Troy', from the Celtic word *Tro*, to turn. The Galatian Celts were, of course, familiar with ancient Troy or Ilion.

In search of serpent-dragons, and monsters of the id, we keep spiralling downwards and inwards, to the subaquatic, subterranean regions of physical and psychical worlds. Once tickled, the monsters rise from the depths to display themselves, sometimes rampantly. Phallic standing stones, thrusting skywards like giant stinkhorns through the earth's surface, seem to symbolize the potent serpent power.

Lewis Carroll made an 'underground' joke about Pat the Irish gardener 'digging for apples'. The apple is the fruit of the Celtic 'Otherworld', closely associated with Hallowe'en. It is also the fruit of Aphrodite. Carroll may have been thinking of a *pomme de terre*, or 'earth apple', the potato, with its Hibernian associations. The name Murphy springs to mind, linking Carroll with yet another Irish stout, as well as Beamish and Guinness. If you think that far-fetched, consider the word 'potatory', meaning boozing, from the Latin *potare*, to drink. A pint of Murphy, Beamish or Guinness stout is a potation, as is a glass of poteen (distilled from potatoes). Have you seen what seed potatoes do in the dark?

Mokele-mbembe, the Congo dinosaur-like mystery creature,

is said to be fond of an apple-like fruit, *molombo*, which grows in the swamps of the Likouala region. During the winter of 1985/6, in a purely advisory and long-distance invocatory capacity, I was involved with Operation Congo, a British *Mokele-mbembe*-seeking expedition. I advised the leader, Bill Gibbons, to take plenty of Guinness and to mark his camera equipment with a special sign, now known as the Nnidnidiogram. For various reasons, Operation Congo turned out to be something of a disaster. Deep in the jungle, feeling rather low, Bill was converted to Christianity. Unfortunately, this sort of thing can happen to the nicest people. Christians associate an apple-like fruit and the serpent-dragon with temptation, original sin, the Fall.

'Phall if you but will, rise you must' says Joyce in the *Wake*.

Young girls used to play a game called 'Humpty Dumpty'. Alice met the egg-man in Looking Glass Land. The magnetic W.C. Fields once played the part. Eggstraordinary. A serpent encircles the Cosmic Egg. Dodgson used albumen in his photographic experiments. Coruscating clues.

The first issue of *Nnidnid*, the magazine, came out during the summer of 1986, containing an article by me on *The Nnidnidification of Ness*, stressing the importance of signs and images in the raising of monsters. Guinness featured Nessie in some of their posters [see pl. 20]. I just knew they would, sooner or later. After the night of Samhain that year, I finally retired from the monster-raising game, once and for all. The beasties had gobbled up far too much of my precious time. Now I wanted to nnidnidify other things. The monster-raising game is, quite obviously, always wide open, and should any readers of this little book wish to try their luck, I would earnestly encourage them to step right up and have a go.

I do not insist, like Sherlock Holmes, that you should apply my methods to the game, but would greatly advise any would-be players to...

Fill your minds with monstrous images and ideas. Use some kind of nnidnidiogram whenever and wherever it seems applicable. Wear a tall hat, stovepipe or steeply conical. Juggle with apples, potatoes and eggs. Scry spirally in the dark depths of Irish stout. Pick bunches of dragonwort. Try spotting uncanny things in mirrors. Think of photography as alchemy. Play golf as a kind of geomancy. Bang a drum. Employ sky-clad witches, respectfully. Experiment with automatic writing and drawing. Practise oneiromancy. Untame your eyes. Indulge in occasional troglodytic pursuits. Read between the lines between the lines. Look at Arcimboldo, himself. Laugh maniacally. Study cephalopods. Explore labyrinths. Learn to recognize magic circumstance and objective chance. Ride a horse. Wear silver and copper objects. Believe absolutely that you can cause unusual happenings. Eat some

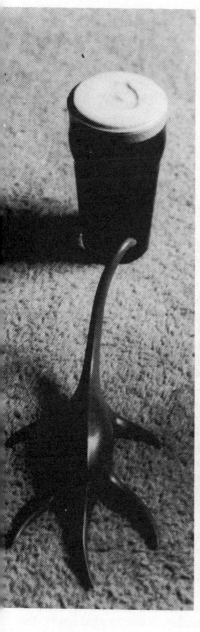

Guinnidnidness!

aphrodisiac molluscs. Go for a swim.

It is now the middle of 1987 and I have written quite enough of this book. My immediate plan is to stroll down to Mr Dermot Maguire's public house and enjoy a pint of his most excellent stout. Then.. ah then...

Nnidnid!!!

Bibliography
& Index!

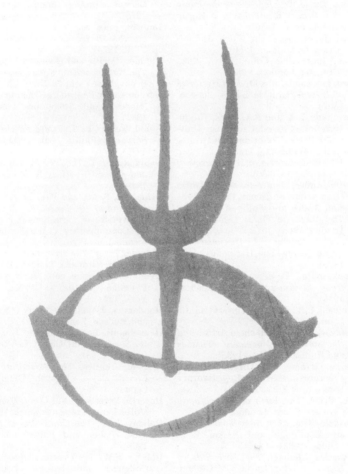

BIBLIOGRAPHY

Allain, Marcel and Pierre Souvestre, *Fantômas* (Pan Books, London, 1987).

Anderson, Alan Orr and Marjorie Ogilvie (ed. and trans.), *Adamnan's Life of Columba* (Thomas Nelson, Edinburgh, 1961).

Binns, Ronald with R.J. Bell, *The Loch Ness Mystery Solved* (Open Books, Somerset, 1983).

Bohm, David, *Wholeness and the Implicate Order* (Routledge and Kegan Paul, London, 1980).

Bord, Janet and Colin, *Alien Animals* (Granada, London, 1980).

Bord, Janet and Colin, *Earth Rites* (Granada, London, 1982).

Bord, Janet and Colin, *Modern Mysteries of Britain* (Grafton Books, London, 1987).

Borradaile, L.A. and F.A. Potts, *The Invertebrata* (4th ed. Cambridge University Press, Cambridge, 1961).

Bottrell, William, *Traditions and Heathside Stories of West Cornwall* (Penzance, 1870-80).

Breton, Andre, *Manifestos of Surrealism* (Ann Arbor, Michigan, 1969).

Breton, André and Philippe Soupault, *The Magnetic Fields* (Atlas Press, London, 1985).

Briggs, Katherine, *A Dictionary of Fairies* (Allen Lane, Harmondsworth, 1976).

Brookesmith, Peter (ed.), *Creatures from Elsewhere* (Orbis, London, 1985).

Cammell, C.R., *Aleister Crowley* (N.E.L., London, 1969).

Chadwick, Whitney, *Women Artists and the Surrealist Movement* (Thames and Hudson, London, 1985).

Clarke, Jerome and Loren Coleman, *Creatures of the Outer Edge* (Warner Books, New York, 1978).

Coe, Brian, *The Birth of Photography* (Ash and Grant, London, 1976).

Dinsdale, Tim, *Loch Ness Monster* (4th ed. Routledge and Kegan Paul, London, 1982).

Edwardes, Michael, *The Dark Side of History* (Hart-Davis McGibbon, London, 1978).

Farson, Daniel, *The Man Who Wrote Dracula* (Michael Joseph, London, 1975).

Finlay, Ian, *Celtic Art: An Introduction* (Faber and Faber, London, 1973).

Fort, Charles Hoy, *The Complete Books of Charles Fort* (Dover, New York, 1974).

Freud, Sigmund, *The Interpretation of Dreams* (Pelican, Harmondsworth, 1985).

Freud, Sigmund, *Art and Literature* (Pelican, Harmondsworth, 1986).

Gasson, Roy (ed.), *The Illustrated Lewis Carroll* (Jupiter Books, London, 1978).

Godwin, John, *Super Psychic: The Incredible Dr. Hoy* (Pocket Books, New York, 1974).

Goldner, Orville and George E. Turner, *The Making of King Kong* (Ballantine Books, New York, 1975).

Gordon, Colin, *Beyond the Looking Glass* (Hodder and Stoughton, London, 1982).

Gould, Rupert T., *The Case for the Sea Serpent* (Phillip Allan, London, 1930).

Gould, Rupert T., *The Loch Ness Monster and Others* (Geoffrey Bles, London, 1934).

Grimshaw, Roger and Paul Lester, *The Meaning of the Loch Ness Monster* (University of Birmingham, Centre for Contemporary Cultural Studies, Birmingham 1976).

Haining, Peter, *The Irish Leprechaun's Kingdom* (Granada, London, 1981).

Helmholtz, Herman von, *Handbook of Physiological Optics* (Dover, New York, 1963).

Henderson, Isobel, *The Picts* (Thames and Hudson, London, 1967).

Heuvelmans, Bernard, *In the Wake of the Sea Serpents* (Rupert Hart-Davis, London, 1968).

Higham, Charles, *The Adventures of Conan Doyle* (Hamish Hamilton, London, 1976).

Hogarth, Peter with Val Clery, *Dragons* (Allen Lane, Harmondsworth, 1979).

Holiday, F.W., *The Great Orm of Loch Ness* (Faber and Faber, London, 1968).

Holiday, F.W., *The Dragon and the Disc* (Sidgwick and Jackson, London, 1973).

Holiday, F.W., *The Goblin Universe* (Llewellyn Publications, St Paul, Minn. 1986).

Hudson, Derek, *Lewis Carroll: An Illustrated Biography* (Constable,

London, 1976).

Hunt, Robert, *Popular Romances of the West of England* (Chatto and Windus, London, 1930).

Huxley, Francis, *The Dragon* (Thames and Hudson, London, 1981).

Iles, Norman, *Who Really Killed Cock Robin* (Robert Hale, London, 1986).

Jaguer, Edouard, *Les Mystères de la Chambre Noir* (Flammarion, Paris, 1982).

Joyce, James, *Finnegans Wake* (Faber and Faber, London, 1939).

Jung, Carl Gustav and others, *Man and His Symbols* (Aldus books, London, 1964).

Keel, John A., *The Mothman Prophecies* (E.P. Dutton, New York, 1975).

Lane, F.W., *Kingdom of the Octopus* (Jarrold, London, 1957).

Lautréamont, Comte de, *Les Chants de Maldoror* (La Boetie, Brussels, 1948).

Leach, Robert, *The Punch and Judy Show* (Batsford, London, 1985).

Lee, Henry, *Sea Monsters Unmasked* (William Clowes, London, 1884).

McEwan, Graham J., *Mystery Animals of Britain and Ireland* (Robert Hale, London, 1986).

Michell, John and Robert J.M. Rickard, *Phenomena: A Book of Wonders* (Thames and Hudson, London, 1977).

Michell, John and Robert J.M. Rickard, *Living Wonders: Mysteries and Curiosities of the Animal World* (Thames and Hudson, London, 1982).

Morgan, Elaine, *The Aquatic Ape* (Souvenir Press, London, 1982).

Morton, J.E., *Molluscs* (Hutchinson, London, 1979).

Nicolaisen, W.F.H., *Scottish Place Names: Their Study and Significance* (Batsford, London, 1976).

Nixon, Marion and B.J. Messenger (eds.),

The Biology of Cephalopods (Zoological Society, London, 1977).

Opie, Iona and Peter, *The Oxford Dictionary of Nursery Rhymes* (Oxford University Press, Oxford, 1969).

Passeron, René, *Phaidon Encyclopedia of Surrealism* (Phaidon, London, 1978).

Penrose, Roland, *Scrapbook* (Thames and Hudson, London, 1981).

Rosenberg, Samuel, *Naked is the Best Disguise* (Arlington Books, London, 1975).

Secrest, Meryle, *Salvador Dali: The Surrealist Jester* (Weidenfield and Nicolson, London, 1986).

Sibley, Brian, *The Book of Guinness Advertising* (Guinness Books, London, 1985).

Simpson, W. Douglas, *Urquhart Castle* (H.M.S.O., Edinburgh, 1976).

Spies, Werner, *Max Ernst. Loplop. The Artist's Other Self* (Thames and Hudson, London, 1983).

Swire, Otta, *The Highlands and Their Legends* (Oliver and Boyd, Edinburgh, 1963).

Tremayne, Peter, *The Curse of Loch Ness* (Sphere, London, 1979).

Tremayne, Peter, *The Morgow Rises* (Sphere, London, 1982).

Wainwright, Frederick T. (ed.), *The Problem of the Picts* (Nelson, Edinburgh, 1955).

Wedeck, H.E, *Dictionary of Gypsy Life and Lore* (Peter Owen, London, 1973).

Wentz, W.Y. Evans, *The Fairy Faith in Celtic Countries* (Oxford University Press, Oxford, 1911).

Whitlock, Ralph, *Here Be Dragons* (Allen and Unwin, London, 1983).

Wilson, Colin and others, *West Country Mysteries* (Bossiney Books, Bodmin, 1985).

PERIODICALS:

FORTEAN TIMES: A Journal of Strange Phenomena: 20 Paul St, Frome, Somerset BA11 1DX. Editors: Mike Dash, Bob Rickard and Paul Sieveking.

FOLKLORE FRONTIERS: 5 Egton Drive, Seaton Carew, Hartlepool, Cleveland, TS25 2AT. Editor: Paul Screeton.

NESSLETTER: Huntshieldford, St Johns Chapel, Bishop Aukland, Co. Durham, DL13 1RQ. Editor: Rip Hepple.

NNIDNID: Surreality: 3 Vale View, Ponsanooth, Truro, Cornwall. Editors: Gareth Shiels and Tony 'Doc' Shiels.

INDEX

Italicized entries are titles of books, paintings, films, etc. A ★ indicates a witness or sighting. Proper names of gods, entities, monsters etc are included, except for 'Nessie' and 'Morgawr'; the whole book concerns them. Italic page numbers refer to illustrations – bold to plates.

Aberdeen *Press and Journal* – 74.
Adamnan – 70.
Adkin, Mrs J.C. – ★ 28.
Agar, Eileen – 97.
Alice – 48, 102-3, 106, *106*, 132. (See also Alice Liddell).
Alice in Wonderland – 16, 104, *106*, 107.
Alice in Wonderland (film, 1933) – 100.
Alice's Adventures Under Ground – 103.
Alice through the Looking Glass – 99.
Alice, Where art thou? – 102.
Alien Animals – 17, 80.
'Amanda' – 32-3, 58.
Andrew – 54-5.
Antana – 21, 1288.
Aphrodite – 133.
Apol – 13-4.
Apollo – 22.
Apophis – 21.
Aquatic Ape, The – 113.
Aragon, Louis – 97, 99.
Arnold, Holly – **21B**.
Artemis – 39.
Artio – 39.
Arthur, King – 39, 132.
Arts Theatre, Falmouth – 80.
Au Rendez-vous des Amis – 99.

Bang, John Kendrick – 103.
Bard, Joseph – 97.
Barrie, James M. – 104.
Batten, J.D. – *24*.
Baudelaire – 132.
BBC TV – 55, 57, 69, 89, 122, **8B**.

Beach, Cyprian – 133.
Beach, Sylvia – 133.
Beast with Five Fingers, The – 91.
Bede – 127.
Bell, Anthony J. – 104.
Bell, J. Mackintosh – ★ 103.
Bell, Joseph.
Bell, Wendy – 104.
Bell and Howell – 104.
Bellerophon – 104.
Benchley, David – 76.
Bennett, Gerald – ★ 28-9, 69.
Benson, Roy – ★ 74.
Big Bird – 52.
Binns, Ronald – 108.
Bird, Sheila and Eric – ★ 130, 132.
Blee, Tammy – 31.
Bohm, David – 108.
Boiffard, Jacques-André – 108.
Bolster – 39.
Bononcini – 102.
Book of Lismore, The – 85.
Bord, Janet and Colin – 17, 77, 80.
Borradaile and Potts – 116.
Bougainville – 123.
Bradbury, Ray – 72.
Breton, André – 37, 40-1, 69, *89*, 99, 101, 103, 131.
Brigid, – 21,69.
'Brigid' – 58.
British Goblins, – *89*.
Broichan – 128.
Brude mac Maelchon – 70, 73, 128.
Bruno, Giordano – 133.
Buñuel, Luis – 77, 127.
Byron, Lord – 16.

Campbell, Alex – ★ 71.
Campbell, Ken – 77.
Campbell, Murdo – 72.
Campbell, Nessie – 104.
Carberry, Georgina – ★ 86.
Carrington, Leonora – 38, 97, *63*.
Carroll, Kitty – 57.
Carroll, Lewis – see Charles Dodgeson.
Case for the Sea Serpent, The – 11.
Celtic Fairy Tales – *24*.
Cernunnos – 21, 32.
Chambers, John – ★ 58
Chants de Maldoror, Les – 130.
Chapman, Sally – ★ 58-9, *59*.
Clarke, David – ★ 64-5, 74-5, **7**.
Cock, John – ★ 62.
Coleridge, Samuel T. – 16.
Coming of the Fairies, The – 99.
Cooper, Gary – 100, 107.
Cooper, Alice – 107.
Cormelian – 39.
Cormoran – 39.
Cornish Life – 62, 64, 74.
Costello, Peter – 85.
Cousteau, Jacques – 122.
Coye, Lee Brown – 130.
Creagh, Seamus – 87-8.
Crosby, Bing – 101.
Crowe, Rich – 90.
Crowley, Aleister – 71, 90, 99, 101.
Crowley, Mike – 111.
Crowther, Pat – 31.
Cthulhu – 131.

Cumin − ★ 28.
*Curse of Loch Ness,
The* − 133.

Daily Mirror − 75 *76*.
Dali, Salvador − 91-2,
101, 122.
Dame Ovale, La − *63*.
Daniel − 128.
Dee, John − 90, 101.
Dinsdale, Tim − 58, 70,
75-7, **18A**.
Distant Humps − 77, **5**.
Dodds, Pauline − 88.
Dodgson, Charles
Lutwidge − 98-100,
102-7, *106*, 111,
132-4, **14A**.
Dolan, Patrick − ★ 62.
Donn − 93.
Doyle, Sir Arthur
Conan − 99, 101, ★
103-4, 107.
*Dragon and the Disc,
The* − 11, 17, 90.
Dracula − 107, 132-3.
Drees, Ashley − 85.
Dunwich Horror, The −
131.
Durham, Frank − 77.

Earwicker − 37.
*Écriture Automatique,
L'* − 99.
Eluard, Paul and Nusch
− 97.
Entrée des Mediums −
99.
Epona − 128.
Ernst, Max − *47*, 59, *60*,
63, 80, 97-9, *98*, 103,
124, 127, *129*, **13B**,
13C.
Exaltation of Larks, An
−101.
Exotic Zoology − 11.

'F, Mary' − ★ 30-1, 91,
112, **6**.
Fabricius, Georgius −
128.
Fairbank, Chris − **5**.
Fairies of all kinds −
see Little People.
Falmouth Packet − 28
-31, 59, 61-2, 130, **5**.

Fantômas −132-33.
Farson, Dan − 107.
Femme 100 Têtes, La −
47, *127*.
Ferris, Donald − 62.
Feuillade, Louis −
132-3.
Field Museum of
Natural History,
Chicago − 116, 118.
Fields, W.C. − 101, 134.
Figgy, Madgy − 31.
Final Problem, The
−103.
Finlay, Greta and
Harry − ★ 122.
Finnegan's Wake − 37,
132-4.
Flecker, James Elroy −
21.
Fleming, Mr and Helen
− ★ 69.
Fort, Charles Hoy − 15,
37-9, 57, 113, 127,
132, **13A**.
Fortean Times − 111,
123, 131.
Fox-Talbot, − W. Henry
− 98, 106, 128.
Freud, Sigmund − 48,
102, 105, 107-8.
Friedricks, H. 118.

*Gallavant Variations,
The* − 80.
Gardner, Gerald − 31.
Garuda − 52.
Gasson, Roy − 102.
Geller, Uri − 66, 91,
107.
Gerber, Neva − 132.
Gibbons, Bill − 134.
Gilbert, Mr − ★ 28.
Gilfeather, Martin − 75.
Glasgow *Daily Record*
− 75-6.
Goblin Universe, The
13-4.
Goddard, Sir Victor −
14.
Golden Dawn − 15.
Goodyear − 108 **18B**.
Gould, Rupert T. − 11,
105, 130.
Gray, Hugh − ★ 72,
120, **16A**.

*Great Orm of Loch
Ness, The* − 11, 116.
Greenwood, Jane − ★
59-61.
Griffiths, Frances − 57,
15A.
Grimshaw, Roger −
108.
Ground Saucer Watch
− 77.
Groves-Raines, Antony
− 102.
Guinness, Arthur and
Sons − 100-1, 105.

Halstead, Jenny − ★
130.
Handel − 102.
Hargreaves, Reginald −
100.
Harpies − 52.
Harrison, Michael − 31.
Harrison, Vernon − 77,
79.
Hayyam, Jabar ibn −
127.
Helmholtz, Hermann
von − 61.
Henry, Charlotte − 100.
Hepple, Rip − 75.
Herakles − 70, 128.
Herne − 128.
Heuvelmans, Bernard −
11, 120, 130.
Higham, Charles − 104.
*Highlands and their
Legends, The* − 101.
Highton, E. − ★ 28.
Hitler, Adolf − 101.
Hodson, Geoffrey −
15A.
Holiday, F.W. 'Ted' −
11-3, 17, 85, 90, 116,
21B.
Holmes, Bramwell − ★
62.
'Holmes, Gordon' − see
M.P. Shiel.
Holmes, Sherlock − 48,
99, 103, 107, 132,
134, **20B**.
Homer − 128.
Hopley, P. − ★ 28.
Hopley, Ray − ★ 69.
Hoy, David − 69, 80,
12A.

Houdini, Harry – 99, 105.
Houdini and Conan Doyle – 104.
Huebner, Louise – 31.
Hunt, Robert – 31, 39, 56.
Hunting of the Snark, The – 99.
Huson, Paul – 32.

Illustrated Lewis Carroll, The – 102.
Innes, Bob – 56.
In the Wake of the Sea Serpent – 11.
Inverness Courier – 71.
Invertebrata, The – 116.
Isidore of Seville – 127.
'Isobel' – 58.
Isaiah – 51.

Jacobs, J. – *24.*
Janus – 38.
Jenkyns, Mr and Mrs – ★ 122.
Jimmy the Wizard – 31.
Johnson, Amelia – 29.
Johnson, Donald – 111.
Joplin, Janis – 38.
Joplin, Scott – 38.
Joyce, James – 15, 37, 103, 132-4.
Judex – 133.
Jung, Carl G. – 16, 102, 105.

Kadirgama, Admiral R. – 111-12, *111.*
Keel, John A. – 13-4, 17, 133.
Kelley, Edward – 90.
Kelley, O'Talbot Laurence – 90, 107.
Kelley, Patrick O'Talbot – ★ 90-1, 107, 112, **22A.**
Kelpie – 128.
Kennedy, Patrick – 85.
Kingdom of the Octopus, The 120.
King Kong – 101, 105-7.
King, Martin Luther – 13.

Lair of the White Worm, The – 107, 133.
Lambton, John – 23.
Lambton Worm, The – 23.
Lane, Frank – 120.
Lautréamont, Compt de – 40, 103, 130.
Leary, Timothy – 31.
Lee, Alice – ★ 130, 132.
Lee, Henry – 130.
Leek, Sybyl – 31.
Legendary Fictions of the Irish Celts, The – 85.
Leland, Charles – 31.
Leslie, Lionel – **21B.**
Lester, Paul – 108.
Lethbridge, T.C. – 31.
Ley, Willy – 11.
Liddell, Arthur – 104.
Liddell, Alice Pleasance – 98-100, 102, **14B.**
Liddell, Dean – 98-9.
Lilitu – 52.
Lindsay, Miss M. – ★ 69, 9.
Lipton, James – 101.
Littérature – 99.
Little People – 55-7, 80, 88, 99, 104-5, 127, **14, 15.**
Living Wonders – 111, 113.
Loch Ness Mystery Solved, The 108.
Looking Glass, The – 99.
Loplop – 97, *98,* 127.
Lost World, The – 99, 101, 103-4.
Loton – 128.
Lovecraft, Howard Phillips – 131-12.
Lumiere brothers – 98.

Mackay, John and Donaldine – ★ 105.
Macleods of Dunvegan – 100.
'Macleod, Torquil' – ★ 112.
Macumin, Lugne – 70.

Maguire, Dermot and Maeve – 100.
Maldoror – 130, 132.
Manitou – 21.
Mann, Wendy – ★ 89.
Man Ray – 97, 99, 108.
March, Lady Arabella – 107.
Marduk – 21.
Marien, Marcel – 108.
Marine Biology – 118.
Mathers, Samuel Liddell – 99.
Martin, Mr – ★ 89.
Masklyn – 90, **12D.**

Maven, Max – 76, **12B.**
May, Leslie – 69.
McCormick, Michael – 29-30, 51, **12C.**
McEwan, Graham – 86.
McLeod, Alex and Mrs – ★ 69.
M'Cumhail, Fion – 85.
Meaning of the Loch Ness Monster, The – 108.
Meigle Museum, Tayside – *114.*
Melling, June and Vicky – ★ 51-2, *52.*
Mesens, E.L.T. – 97.
Meyer, Nicholas – 107.
Michel, John – 111, 113.
Midgard Serpent – 21.
Mighty Joe Young – 105.
Miller, Lee – 97.
Miller, Penny – *113.*
Milligan, Spike – 15.
Mokele Mbembe – 133-34.
Mollusca – 116.
Moore, Peter – 92.
More, A.G. – 123.
Morgan, Elaine – 113.
Morgan le Fay – 56.
Moriarty, Alice – 103.
Morrigan 56.
Morton, JJ.E. – 116, 122.
Mothman – 14, 52, *52, 59,* 133.
Mothman Prophesies, The – 14, 133.

Munro, Margaret – ★ 112.
Murray, Margaret – 31.
Mussolini – 90-1.
Mystery Ship, The – 131.
Myths and Legends of Southern Africa – 113.

Naked is the Best Disguise – 103.
Nagas – 128.
Nehemiah – 21.
Ness Fisheries Board – 71.
Nessus – 128.
Newquay Colour Services – 74.
New Scientist – 111.
Nidhoggr – 21.
Nnidnid – 127, 130, 134.
Northern Chronicle – 71.
Nougé, Paul – 108.

Obbyoss – 40, 57-8, 132.
O'Brien, Flann – 15.
O'Brien, Willis – 101, 103.
Occult, The – 15.
O'Daly, Peter – 92.
O'Donoghue – 85.
O'Donoghue, Eileen and Mary – 87-8.
Old Joan – 31.
Ollpiast – 85.
Omand, Donald – 12.
Operation Congo – 134.
O'Shaughnessy, Arthur – 85.
O'Shea, Kathleen – ★ 87.
O'Siadhail clan – 85.
Ottewill, T. – 98.
Ouroboros – 21.
Owen, David – 102.
Owlman – Ch.4, *52, 59,* 80, 89, 97, 101, 104, 130-31.

Quetzalcoatl – 21.

Partridge, Eric – 102.

Pat the Irish gardener – 105, 133
Payne, Kay – ★ 29.
Pendragon family – 39.
Pengersick family – 31 10A.
Pengersick, Lady – 27, 102, 107.
Penrose, Roland and 'Beacus' – 97.
Pentreath, Dolly – 27.
Perdurabo – see Aleister Crowley.
Pernetty, Abbé – 123.
Perry, Barbara – ★ 58-9, *59.*
Perseus – 128.
Persistence of Memory, The – 91.
Piasa – 52.
Piers Plowman – 38.
Piggott, Stuart – 40.
Pla, Josef – 92.
Pliny – 120.
Pooka etc – 56, 88.
Poseidon – 128.
Pouakai – 52.
Power, Dennis – 111.
Private Life of Sherlock Holmes, The – 104, **20B.**
PSI (Psychic Seven International) – 69.
'Psyche' – see Pat Scott-Innes.
Puck – 56.
Puck Fair – 87.
Pumphrey, R.J. – 116.
Punch –40, 57, 4.
Purple Cloud, The – 101.
Pursuit of the House Boat, The – 103
Pwca – 88, *89,* 128.
Python – 22.

Ra – 21.
Randi, The Amazing – 107.
Ravensworth, Baron – see Arthur Liddell.
Read, Herbert – 97.
Redgrove, Peterr – 80.
Red-headed League, The – 103.
Reese, Mr – ★ 28.

Richards, Mr – 32.
Richardson, E.S. – 116.
Richardson, Maurice – 107.
Rickard, Robert J.M. – 55, 75, 77, 111, 113, 131.
Ridge Theatre, San Francisco – 77.
Riley, Mr – ★ 28.
Rines, Robert – 13.
Robson, G.C. – 122.
Rogers, Tony – ★ 58.
Rosenberg, Samuel – 103-4.
Royal Photographic Society – 77.
Rutter, Robert – 39.

Sanders, Alex – 31.
Satan – 21.
Schwitters, Kurt – 42.
Scott, Mrs – ★ 28.
Scott, Janet – 38, 55.
Scott-Innes, Pat – 32-3, 38, 46, 54-8, ★ 69.
Scott, Sir Peter – 77.
Scylla – 128.
Sea Monsters Unmasked – 130.
Secombe, Sir Harry – 15.
Semaine de Bonté, Une – *60.*
Shadow, The – 133.
Shakespeare – 101.
Shaw, Sandra – 107.
Shiel, Matthew Phipps – 101.
Shiels family – 128, **5.**
Shiels, Chris – 44, 46, 48, 52, 61, 72-5, 87-8, 92, **4.**
Shiels, Ewan – 81, 87.
Shiels, Gareth – 87, **4.**
Shiels, Kate – 38, 56, 80, 87, 92, **2B, 3B.**
Shiels, Meig – 80, 87-8.
Shiels, Nessie – 104.
Shiels, Thomas D. – 104.
Shiels, Sir Thomas Drummond – 104.
Shine, Adrian – **18B.**
Sikes, Wirt – 89.
Sir Nigel – 101.

Smart, Keenan – 122.
Smith, John – ★ 69.
Smith, Richard and Lynn – ★ 72.
Society of American Magicians – 99.
Solem, G. Alan – 118.
Soupault, Philippe – 69.
Spaulding – 103-4.
Spicer – ★ 28.
Spicer, George – ★ 71, *71*, 105, 112, 122.
Spooks – 77, 107.
St Coemgen – 85.
St Colomba – 70, 127.
St George – 39, 128.
St Mo-Chua – 85.
St Neot – 56.
St Ninian – 127.
St Patrick – 85.
St Seonan – 85.
Steele, David – 102.
Steward, James – 123.
Stoker, Bram – 103, 107, 133.
Sun, The – 80.
Surrealism and Painting – 97, **13C.**
Sutcliffe, Frank – 107.

Swire, Otta – 101.
Sylvie and Bruno – 104, 133.

Talbot, Larry – 107.
Táin bo Cuailgne – 43.
Tengu – 52.
Terry, Ellen – 107.
Thatcher, Margaret – 91, 97.
That Obscure Object of Desire – 77.
Tiamat – 21.
Tolkein, J.R.R. – 31.
Tomfool's Theatre of Tomfoolery – 57, 81.
Trecrobben – 38.
Tremaine, Peter – 133.
Truscott, Mike – 75.

Ubac, Raoul – 108.
Updike, John – 91.

Vallée, Jacques – 13, 17.
Varo, Remedios – 38.
Vampires, Les – 133.
Venerable Game, The – 101.
Viner, Duncan – ★ 29.

Vinnecombe, George – 62.
Vishnu – 21.
'Vivienne' – 32-3, 55.
Voss, Gilbert L. – 122.

Water Horse – 128.
Western Morning News – 28.
Westward TV – 12.
White, Alan and Sally – ★ 64.
White Stains – 99.
Wilkins, Harold T. – ★ 28.
Wilson, Ben – 132.
Wilson, Kepple and Betty – 32.
Wilson, Robert Anton – 105.
'Witch of Fraddam, The' – 31.
'Witch of Treva', The – 31.
Wolfman, The – 107.
Wray, Fay – 105-6.
Wright, Elsie – 57, **15.**

Yggdrasil – 21.
Yog-Sothoth – 131.
Young, J.. – 120, 122.